Leslie,

Be joyful and live out your dreams!

JOYFUL LIVING

Liên Ngũ

Made for Success Publishing
P.O. Box 1775 Issaquah, WA 98027
www.MadeForSuccess.com

Copyright © 2024. All rights reserved.

In accordance with the U.S. Copyright Act of 1976, the scanning, uploading, and electronic sharing of any part of this book without the permission of the publisher constitutes unlawful piracy and theft of the author's intellectual property. If you would like to use material from the book (other than for review purposes), prior written permission must be obtained by contacting the publisher at service@madeforsuccess.net. Thank you for your support of the author's rights.

Distributed by Blackstone Publishing

First Printing

Library of Congress Cataloging-in-Publication data

Liên Ngū
    Joyful Living
        p. cm.

LCCN: 2024944415
ISBN: 978-1-64146-884-8 (*Paperback*)
ISBN: 978-1-64146-886-2 (*eBook*)
ISBN: 978-1-64146-885-5 (*Audiobook*)

Printed in the United States of America

For further information, contact Made for Success Publishing
+1(425) 526-6480 or email service@madeforsuccess.net

*To my three K.I.D.s – Kaitlynn, Iris, and Derek –
whose laughter and love fill my days with joy.
I hope this book serves as a guiding light for you,
helping you to embrace and live a joyful life.
May the lessons within inspire you as you grow
and carry them with you always.*

*And to my husband, Hao Dang,
whose unwavering support made
this journey possible.
Thank you for being my partner
in this joyful adventure.*

Table of Contents

Introduction 1

PART 1 FINDING HAPPINESS

Chapter 1 Defining Happiness 9

Chapter 2 Look Within Yourself 13

Chapter 3 Adjust Your Perspective
to Avoid Suffering 17

Chapter 4 You and the Universe:
Co-creators of Your Life 21

Chapter 5 Compulsive vs Conscious 25

Chapter 6 Unhappiness is the Gap Between
Expectations and Reality 29

Chapter 7 The Battle Between
Happiness and Ego 31

Chapter 8 How Happiness Can Help Us
          Get What We Want.. 35

Chapter 9 Share Your Gift with the World 39

PART 2 THE LAW OF ATTRACTION (LOA)

Chapter 10 The Law of Attraction 45

Chapter 11 Step 1: Ask 47

Chapter 12 Step 2: It is Given.............................. 55

Chapter 13 Step 3: Allow 59

Chapter 14 Step 4: Embrace Contrast................. 67

Chapter 15 Summary of LOA............................. 75

PART 3 HAPPINESS HABITS

Chapter 16 Miracle Morning 81

Chapter 17 AID (Appreciation,
            Intention, Delegation)......................... 87

Chapter 18 Meditation and Mindfulness 95

Chapter 19 Use Your Brain's Resources Well 103

Chapter 20 Job, Career, or Calling....................... 107

Chapter 21 Bring Your Energy Up...................... 111

PART 4 HAPPY RELATIONSHIPS

Chapter 22 Our Need for Relationships 119

Chapter 23 The Four Personality Types 123

Chapter 24 FORM 127

Chapter 25 Holding onto Relationships 131

PART 5 CREATING YOUR DESTINY

Chapter 26 Karma 145

Chapter 27 Understanding Karma 153

Chapter 28 How Do You Create Good Karma? 157

Chapter 29 Live Life Consciously 161

Chapter 30 Weathering the Storm 165

Chapter 31 It's Okay to be Angry 173

Chapter 32 The Butterfly Effect 177

Chapter 33 Fulfillment 179

Chapter 34 Real Happiness 183

Chapter 35 Conclusion 185

Introduction

WHAT DO YOU want in life? Joy? Money? Fame?

We are all looking for something in life. So, before we begin, please ask yourself these simple questions: What am I missing out on? And what do I think will make me happy?

People often say they will be happy *when* . . . when they get that car, that promotion, that perfect partner, or when they reach that ideal weight. They'll be happy when they leave their current job and find the perfect job. Or when they change spouses, when their kids grow up, or when they make enough money to buy that house. They are always chasing something. If they only achieve *this* particular goal, then they will be happy.

I was also in that "I'll be happy *when* . . ." trap.

All my life, I thought, "I will be happy when I have a corporate job in a high rise." Little did I know that when I finally got there, I would work not 9-to-5 but sometimes

9-to-9. Then, I thought, "If I get out of this boring job, a new job will be more interesting and challenging." After two or three years, I was bored again. The excitement and happiness faded. And then I thought again, "If I can find another company to work for, then I'll be happy." I found out that the grass is *not* greener on the other side. It was the same politics, the same workload, and the same type of work. Something was missing.

While I was chasing after each new goal, I left some people behind, including myself. I didn't know who I was anymore. "The happily ever after" never came. I felt empty inside. When I reached one goal, I started looking for the next thing, which, it turned out, was not that promising. I started questioning my life and existence. I began to wonder what I was working so hard for.

I thought about my life and started to really wonder what life was all about. What would make me happy? One of my biggest dreams was to have kids and live in a beautiful home with good schools and neighbors. I also wanted to be a spiritual teacher, and all in all, I wanted to be happy. As I was searching for this happiness, I came across a class called Destiny by Design. This class taught me about the Law of Attraction. I learned that what you focus on, you attract. Your feelings are your ultimate attractor, so you have to feel good to attract good things. This changed the way I live my life.

My goal was—and is—to have a lasting impact and help others learn what I learned. One of my mentors asked me, "Why do you have to wait until you have a huge following or be on a big stage to be a spiritual speaker? You can do it right now, with the people around you first. Start small, and eventually, you'll get there." So, I started doing small talks at my temple and hosted small groups with my friends. Through those talks, one of the audience members liked my speech and even invited me to be a guest speaker for the Taiwanese American Professional National Conference in Seattle. Since my self-discovery journey, I have helped many people become happier. Utilizing my principles and strategies, people have been able to apply what they learned and create the joyful life they want!

In my personal life, I have reached my goal of having not only one but three children. I have a loving husband, and we bought our dream home in a neighborhood that I love. I feel very blessed to have discovered this path of living life with joy. My life is fulfilling every day, even though I still have goals and dreams to pursue. I am joyfully working toward my goals. As my mentor says, "Appreciate what you have and be eager for more!"

We think that when we achieve something important, we will feel happy. But we often forget to enjoy the journey along the way. We forget to appreciate the struggles, the people who supported us, and the journey itself. We forget to appreciate the little things in life, which require us to be present.

In his book *The Power of Now*, spiritual author Eckhart Tolle explores the idea that the past is over, and the future is not here. The only reality is the present moment. Tolle argues that we must embrace the here and now to fully experience life. Our life's purpose is to enjoy the experience, accept who we are, appreciate all there is, and be present in the now. There is never a time when your life is not "this moment."

Tolle shared a story that speaks to the importance of "the now" in a very profound way. Tolle recounts the story of a beggar who, for thirty years, sat on a wooden box by the roadside, asking people for money.

One day, he asked a stranger, "Spare some change?"

"Sorry, I don't have anything to give you," the stranger replied. "What are you sitting on?"

"Nothing, just an old box," the beggar said, hanging his head.

"Ever look inside?"

"No, what's the point? There's nothing inside."

"Let's have a look together, shall we?" the stranger said, motioning for the beggar to stand up.

The beggar managed to pry it open, and to his surprise, he found gold. The beggar was shocked. All this time, he had been sitting on a treasure box full of gold, never once thinking to look inside.[1]

Think of me as the stranger in this story. What I have to offer is the suggestion that you look inside yourself. Find the treasure in your life.

Introduction

You might be thinking, "But I'm not a beggar. What does this have to do with me?"

For anyone who hasn't yet found true wealth—pure joy, peace, and love—you are a beggar. In fact, even if you have all the material wealth in the world—a huge house, a thriving business, and expensive cars—if you don't possess happiness, you're still lost. The external things are fleeting; they are simply pleasure, not true happiness. As the Tibetan saying goes, "Seeking happiness outside ourselves is like waiting for sunshine in a cave facing north." What we need to do is look inside ourselves.

Once we can wrap our minds around the fact that happiness is within, we can start to see the wonder in every little thing around and inside of us. Every time we see a giggling baby or a young child playing, we're reminded that we are all born with a natural and innate sense of happiness. Joy is actually our birthright!

In this book, I want to help you find happiness from the inside out by appreciating the small and big moments so you can weather any storm that comes your way. When you take time to work on yourself and align with who you really are—your true self—your problems will start to fall away, and happiness will be easily accessible. I will be sharing advice, exercises, and practices you can do daily to adjust your mindset and live a joyful life.

PART 1
FINDING HAPPINESS

Chapter 1

DEFINING HAPPINESS

IN MY EXPERIENCE as a parent, children wake up happy; they're joyful almost all the time. Why? They don't get mad over little things. When you see kids walking around, they're skipping, carefree.

As we grow older, many of us find ourselves burdened by the weight of responsibilities, leading to a palpable sense of unhappiness. The joy of childhood often gives way to the monotony of adult life, where obligations like work, errands, and the relentless hustle overshadow the simple pleasures that once brought us joy. This shift can create a mindset where we focus on "having to" rather than "getting to," diminishing our appreciation for the richness of life. The pressures of daily demands can lead to feelings of stress and exhaustion, causing us to walk through life with our heads down and shoulders hunched as if carrying an invisible load. We may forget that life is a precious gift, filled with opportunities for joy and connection. The challenge lies in reclaiming that sense of wonder and gratitude, reminding ourselves that happiness is not just a distant goal but a choice we can make each day, regardless of our circumstances.

So, what is happiness, and how do we achieve it?

As you can imagine, there has been plenty of research on happiness. Some of my favorite research on the topic is from Shawn Achor's research at Harvard University. His research enabled him to write his book, *The Happiness Advantage*. Achor spent a significant amount of time proving that there's a real advantage to being happy. In addition to conducting research, he also taught a course at Harvard called Happiness 101. At the time, there were more students enrolled in that class than there were in economics—that should tell you something about what people are actually interested in learning. Like most of us, Harvard students are looking for happiness; they want to learn everything they can about it and how to obtain it.

I love Achor's definition of happiness from *The Happiness Advantage*: "Happiness is the joy you feel moving toward your potential."[1]

The majority of us have likely been told that if we work hard enough, we will be successful, and thus, we will become happy. However, as Achor points out, it's actually the opposite. We must be happy in order to achieve success and maximize our potential.[2]

How can that be? Well, when we are happy—when our mindset and mood are positive—we are more motivated and, thus, more successful.

Think about a time when you were truly happy. Didn't you feel like you could accomplish anything? Didn't you have more energy, as if you could run a 5K if you wanted to? Didn't you feel inspired, bursting to the brim with creativity?

So, I pose this question to you: What lens are you looking through? Just like the "glass half full or half empty" adage, life is all about how you perceive it. If you focus on the negative, you will get negative results. If you focus on the positive, positive things will happen in your life.

To know true happiness, you must first shift your mindset to view your life through a positive lens. Then, success will follow, and you will realize your full potential.

Chapter 2

LOOK WITHIN YOURSELF

IMAGINE THIS SCENARIO: For the past couple of weeks, you've been noticing that you feel aches and pains, you've had a hard time sleeping, and you are a bit off. So, you go to the doctor and share your list of symptoms with her, hoping she can figure out what is going wrong. The doctor takes some notes and writes a few prescriptions for you. She hands them to you and says, "You're all done for the day!"

As you look through the prescriptions, you realize that none of them are for medication for you. They are for other people in your life. Some are for your mom, your spouse, your employees, your boss, your clients, your in-laws, and so on.

Obviously, relying on external circumstances or the behavior of others to dictate our happiness is a flawed approach. While kindness from others can enhance our experiences, waiting for external validation or change is not a sustainable solution. People are complex, and their actions are influenced by their own struggles and circumstances. Expecting others to validate us puts our happiness in their hands, which can lead to disappointment and frustration.

Conversely, when we are unhappy, we tend to blame others. "If only my husband would change or my boss would be nicer, then I'd be happy." We blame strangers, coworkers, or our family, but we are looking in the wrong places. To be frank, *we* are the problem. We need to take responsibility for our own lives. The answers to our problems are not somewhere "out there"; rather, the solutions can be found *inside* us.

Most of us have got it all wrong: We are searching for happiness outside of ourselves, and we will keep searching forever because we are looking in all the wrong places. The truth is that happiness is an inside job. This mindset empowers us to reclaim control over our emotions and experiences, fostering resilience and contentment regardless of external influences. Only we can make ourselves happy. If we wouldn't expect the doctor to prescribe us medicine for our spouse to change or our boss to be nicer to solve our physical health problems, then why would we rely on their behavior for our mental health and happiness? If we expect others to make us happy, we will always be disappointed.

Look Within Yourself

True happiness begins within. It requires us to shift our perspective and take responsibility for our emotional well-being. By focusing on our own thoughts, attitudes, and behaviors, we can cultivate an inner sense of joy that isn't contingent on how others treat us. This might involve practicing self-compassion, setting healthy boundaries, and engaging in activities that bring us fulfillment. When we change our mindset and embrace positivity, we radiate that energy outward, often attracting more kindness and positivity from others as a natural consequence. By prioritizing our own growth and happiness, we not only uplift ourselves but also create a more positive environment for those around us.

Chapter 3

ADJUST YOUR PERSPECTIVE TO AVOID SUFFERING

WHY DO PEOPLE suffer? Why are people so unhappy? There are two main reasons: your physical being and your mindset.

We are all familiar with physical pain. Physical pain usually includes easily recognizable things, like a bruised knee or a stomachache. Physical pain is often at the forefront of our minds, and its source is often visible. But what do you do when you can't pinpoint the pain, when it isn't an ache or a wound but something deeper and less detectable?

If we're not physically hurt, but we are in pain, then we're experiencing pain because of our minds. We suffer because of negative thoughts and doubts. We don't think we're good enough. We are jealous, angry, or mad about our past; we think others haven't treated us fairly.

We might be sad because someone left us or our relationship is not going the way we wanted. Maybe there's drama between family members, and they are gossiping about each other. People often complain about what other people are doing instead of what *they* are doing.

With regards to our finances, maybe we're unhappy because of a few zeros missing behind our paycheck or in our bank account. Or the stock market has crashed, and we're upset by the graphs showing our funds going down. This little graph doesn't cause any physical pain or suffering. So why are we so upset?

As you can see, most of the time, everyone is suffering because of their mindset. The truth is that our own thoughts cause us the most suffering. No one can make you suffer. The only thing that's causing you suffering is your mind.

When you are in emotional pain, you are full of negative emotions. All those negative emotions cause you to do all sorts of things. When you can't fight those negative emotions, you might turn to alternatives that will numb you or take away your suffering. Sometimes, people turn to drug use, drinking, or smoking. But using these substances is like putting a Band-Aid on a bullet wound. It may cover it up for a moment, but it doesn't fix anything. These solutions are short-term and futile, and once the substance is gone, you will be back where you were before and possibly even worse off.

I love what Diamond Sutra describes, that our Essence of Mind should not be affected by what we see, hear, taste, touch, or anything we do. We should develop our Essence of Mind so that nothing affects it whatsoever. According to Diamond Sutra, "Our Essence of Mind is essentially our true self, our true nature, or pure mind." Our original pure mind, which is the seed or kernel of enlightenment *[bodhi]*, is pure by nature, and by making use of this mind alone, we can reach Buddhahood directly.

Can you imagine having a bulletproof mind, where nothing can affect you? No matter what people say to you, no matter what happens in the economy or in your family, you would be able to stay positive and find happiness if your mind was bulletproof. So, if you do not let anything bother you or penetrate your positive attitude, you will never, ever suffer. You will be in bliss at all times. You'll be so joyful because nothing bothers you.

If you are struggling to manage your negative thoughts, remember that we often suffer with a negative mindset because we're too close to the problem, and we refuse to take a step back and reassess the situation. Consider this common situation: One day, you are driving home from work, and someone cuts you off. You think, "Oh my goodness, I can't believe he cut me off. That's so rude!" You start to get angry. Then, you continue driving, and you slowly come to a complete stop due to traffic. Again, the negative thoughts take over. "Oh, my goodness, this is so miserable!" So, you experience an hour of misery. You just can't wait to go home, but there is nothing you can do about your situation.

Instead, why not try to enjoy the ride home? It's time to fortify your mind and put your bulletproof shields in place. Don't let your environment or the behavior of other drivers control you. Concentrate on observing the bigger picture. If you zoomed out, you would see that the traffic is actually beautiful from afar. You would see the hustle and bustle of the city or the greenery of the winding suburbs. If you look at the world from afar, it's gorgeous. Take a moment to step back, appreciate the beauty all around you, and just breathe.

If you're serious about achieving true happiness, challenge yourself to confront frustrating situations from this new perspective. You can solve every single problem if you look at it from a larger point of view and with a positive mindset. Anything can be solved if you look from a distance.

Chapter 4

YOU AND THE UNIVERSE: CO-CREATORS OF YOUR LIFE

YOU ARE A co-creator of your life; the other co-creator is the universe.

Every thought that crosses through your mind sends out a vibration. Our minds are like the Internet, posting messages about what we want so the universe can see. Think of it this way: Your mind is the *Inner*net that connects you to the universe.

With that said, if your mind is like the Internet, then what you think about influences how you feel, and what you feel is what you attract. Think of how your social media accounts filter for the things you like so they can show you more of what you want to see. In the same way, your feelings act as a filter for the universe. If you feel good, you will attract good things. Have you ever been in a good mood, and everything seemed to flow easily for you? You hit every green light. You got the job offer you wanted, and you had all this good news come to you. Conversely, when you were feeling bad or crappy, you hit all the red lights, drinks spilled on you, and you just kept hitting a wall. When it rains, it pours!

This is the result of our state of mind. Our emotions have the ability to control everything in our lives: our mood, our decisions, and our actions.

For example, at one point in my life, I knew that I wanted to buy a new car. After doing some research, I narrowed it down to Lexus SUVs. To my surprise, I started to see Lexus SUVs multiple times a day. It's not that they suddenly started driving on the same roads as me, but rather, my focus was on that specific car. They had always been there, but as soon as my mind was focused on buying a Lexus, I started to notice them more. And the more I saw them, the more I wanted one, so I ended up at the Lexus dealership to pull the trigger and buy the car! As Tony Robbins says, "Where focus goes, energy flows."[1]

With that in mind, do you find that you focus more on the negative aspects of your life or the positive? Do you focus on politics, tragedies, disasters, and the friends that hurt you? Or do you spend your time thinking about the good things, like breathing fresh air, living in a free country, and having a roof over your head?

Most people don't get what they want because they focus on what they *don't* want. For example, if they don't make enough money to enjoy all the things they want to enjoy, they focus on the money they don't have and the things they can't do instead of the things they can do.

Each of us has to make the conscious choice to either complain about or appreciate the situation we're in. Think about how drastically your energy would shift if you simply started redirecting your thoughts toward the positive by looking at the bright side of things.

Do you complain about not having enough money, or do you appreciate what you have? Do you focus on the problem or the solution? If things don't go your way, do you start to panic, or do you calmly try to find a solution? When you focus on finding a solution, oftentimes, it presents itself to you simply because you were looking for it.

What you focus on will expand into the universe, and the universe will present it to you. So, be conscious of what you spend your time focusing on.

Chapter 5

COMPULSIVE VS CONSCIOUS

IN ANY GIVEN situation, you can choose to act in one of two ways: compulsively or consciously. Compulsive actions usually have ugly outcomes, while conscious actions are often beautiful.

You are probably familiar with some of the more common compulsive actions. For example, overconsumption of drugs or alcohol, eating until you feel sick, or buying more than you can afford are all compulsive actions. These actions feel good, but they are not sustainable. They often cause ugly results, such as health issues and financial struggles.

If you shift your perspective to being conscious instead of compulsive, you will be able to enjoy some of the same activities that you previously abused. Take shopping, for example. Let's assume that you are a compulsive shopper who enjoys buying gifts for yourself and others due to the instant gratification of each purchase. However, you quickly bury yourself in debt, which causes a lot of emotional and relational problems. You can see how ugly—not to mention scary—this situation would be.

The important thing to note about this situation is not only to be wary of compulsivity but to be conscious of the consequences of your actions, and then be deliberate about what you choose to do next. In this theoretical situation, once you have identified that you have a problem with compulsive shopping, you can be more conscious about your choices surrounding shopping. You can consciously avoid walking by your favorite stores, or you can delete shopping apps from your phone. When you do need to go shopping, you can practice making deliberate and well-thought-out decisions about each item you pick up.

Keep in mind that changing your behavior starts with changing your thoughts and your mindset. You have to change your mindset and believe that you *can* make the change. The mind has immense power. If you don't believe you can change, you won't. So, practice meditating on your vision for your life, focus on the path you want to follow, and then make a plan that aligns with this vision. Remind yourself that you are capable and that this journey will benefit you in the long run.

Once you tame this habit and make it a conscious choice, then each item you buy for yourself will feel like a special treat, and each item you buy for others will still bring them happiness without breaking the bank. In contrast to your previous situation, these acts of generosity and self-care are beautiful and well-balanced.

Of course, being conscious of your thoughts and actions is easier said than done. It takes practice, and sometimes, you will fail. But if you are determined to keep trying, to keep analyzing your choices and doing what is truly best for you and others instead of just doing what you desire at the moment, then you will attract beauty, balance, and good things.

Chapter 6

UNHAPPINESS IS THE GAP BETWEEN EXPECTATIONS AND REALITY

WHEN WE ARE born, we are naturally happy. Kids do not need a fancy car or a nice house to be happy. They are happy beings until they start getting conditioned by the media and outside sources to think they need outside things to be happy. If we are content with what we have, we will not suffer. Most of our unhappiness is caused by the gap between our expectations and our reality.

But how do we close the gap? If our reality doesn't meet our expectations, we either have to lower our expectations, accept our circumstances, or do something about it. My minister, Dr. Lee, always says, "Lower your desires. Don't have so many desires that it's impossible to

Joyful Living

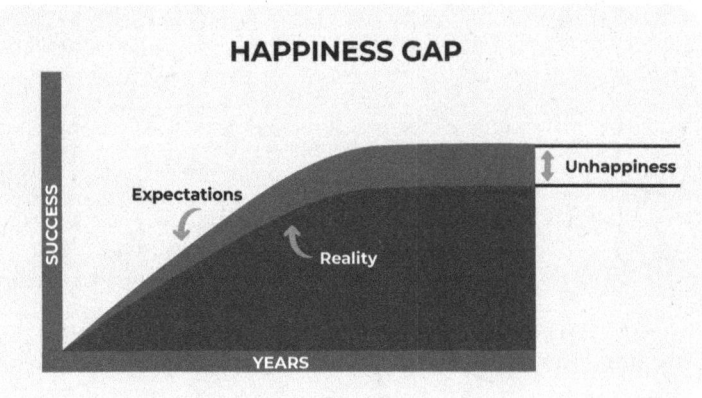

fulfill them." Why desire so much when we can't achieve everything?

Life does not cause suffering, but our expectations of life do cause suffering. For example, if a homeless person has the opportunity to eat dinner at a small family diner, he will be happy because he never expected to go out to eat. A rich person with a home and a good career might go to the same restaurant and be unhappy because he's used to eating at even nicer places. He's not happy because of his expectations. That rich man should just appreciate what's in front of him.

As Tony Robbins says, "Trade your expectation for appreciation, and the world changes instantly!"[1] When you change your mindset and manage your expectations carefully, then your world will shift from revolving around impossible expectations to focusing on appreciation. When you don't feel like you are missing anything, there is nothing missing in your life. You are whole and complete.

Chapter 7

THE BATTLE BETWEEN HAPPINESS AND EGO

SOMETIMES, WE ARE not happy because we try to satisfy our egos instead of seeking true happiness. When I was young, I thought, "I want to work in a high-rise in the corporate world and climb the corporate ladder," but when I got there, it was not that fulfilling. I was like everyone else; I went to school, got a job, and tried to be a manager. I was working long hours and had a poor work-life balance. I was miserable. As I was working, I watched my manager and asked myself, "Is this what I want?" She worked way more hours than me, and I knew how much she got paid because I worked in finance. I said to myself, "I don't know if it's worth it, so what do I want?" This is when I started trying to find what I truly wanted and what made me happy.

Sometimes, what we think we want in life isn't what we really need to be truly happy. Most often, we are trying to feed our ego. Our ego is your "I" or "Self." Ego is how you identify and distinguish yourself from others. In my life, I was feeding my ego, trying to get that "Manager" title so I could identify as a qualified, successful authority figure. In reality, I just wanted to "look good" or impress others, but that is not what makes me truly happy. What I found out later through my self-discovery journey is that I like to learn, grow, and share my findings with others. That is what I am doing now: writing this book, sharing my wisdom daily on social media, and doing monthly talks to help others find their happiness.

People often look for happiness outside themselves due to their ego. Your ego wants to identify with something or someone. People have an image to portray. They try to "look good." That's why they try to impress everyone and themselves. The perception of glamour or material things is an illusion we make up in our minds. We forget the essential fact that underneath our carefully constructed appearances, we are one with all that is.

There is one very important thing our egos try to cover up: the fear of not being whole. People are afraid to be made fun of or humiliated; they are scared of failure and of looking bad. When people do not feel complete or good enough, they try to make themselves feel whole with possessions, status, recognition, a social life, and experiences. They think they are not good enough, so they try to get all these accolades to prove to others that they are good enough. Letting your ego drive your decisions fuels this natural desire as it constantly needs to be fed and protected.

Instead, remember you are perfect just the way you are. You don't have to prove anything. Also, when you are trying to pursue something, think about what you are feeding. Are you feeding your higher self or your ego? Will it make you happy, or is it for other people to "show" them you are good enough or get their approval?

Chapter 8

HOW HAPPINESS CAN HELP US GET WHAT WE WANT

AS I MENTIONED in Chapter 1, Shawn Achor from Harvard University conducted admirable research on happiness. According to Achor, "Happiness is the key to success. Success is not the key to happiness. Most people think that you have to be successful in order to be happy. No, it's actually the opposite. The key to success is happiness."[1]

The most successful people, the ones with a competitive edge, don't view happiness as some distant reward for their achievements, nor do they grind through their days on neutral or negative; they are the ones who capitalize on the positive and reap the rewards at every turn.

Success orbits around happiness, not the other way around. Happiness is the center, and success revolves around it.

In Achor's book *The Happiness Advantage*, he discusses the results of a meta-analysis of happiness research that brought together the results of over two hundred scientific studies of nearly 275,000 people. The analysis found that happiness leads to success in nearly every domain of our lives, including marriage, health, friendship, community involvement, creativity, and, in particular, our jobs, careers, and businesses.[2]

The data showed that happy employees have higher levels of productivity, produce higher sales, perform better in leadership positions, and receive higher performance ratings and higher pay. They also enjoy job security and are less likely to take sick days, quit, or become burnt out.[3]

Achor also suggests that happiness can improve our physical health, which in turn keeps us working faster and longer and, therefore, makes us more likely to succeed. Unhappy employees take more sick days and stay home for an average of 1.25 more days a month, or fifteen extra days a year. Studies have determined that happiness functions as the cause, not just the result, of good health.[4] The list of benefits of being happy goes on and on.

You might wonder: "What if I'm not a happy person?" Anyone can be happy if they work on it. Science has proven that we have far more control over our own emotional well-being than previously believed. While we each have a happiness baseline, we can raise that baseline permanently so that even when there are ups and downs, we are functioning at a higher level.

Chapter 9

SHARE YOUR GIFT WITH THE WORLD

YOU CAN BE successful all you want, but if you don't share it, it can be very lonely and unfulfilling. If you do things that make you happy, the happiness will last for a little while, but when you help others be successful or happy, it will last a lifetime. Each of us has a gift inside us. Our purpose is to find that gift, and once we do, share that gift with the world. If you didn't, it would be like having a cure for cancer and not sharing it. That would be a tragedy. Sadhguru said, "If you do not do what you cannot do, it is all right. But if you do not do what you can do, your life is a tragedy."[1]

I know one thing: Every person on this earth has a gift to share with the world. I saw this video from Prince

Ea about living out your dreams. He once spoke to a pilot about how common the fear of flying is. Most of us hold the notion that flying in an airplane is dangerous. However, the pilot told him that it is actually far more dangerous for a plane to stay on the ground than it is to fly.

"What? How do you mean?" Prince Ea said, shocked.

"Well," the pilot said, "if the plane stays on the ground, it starts to rust, malfunction, and wear out much faster than it would if it was in the air."[2]

What a revelation! Just as planes were built to live in the skies, every person was built to live out the dream they have inside of them. Perhaps the saddest loss of all is to live life on the ground without ever taking off!

So, what dreams do you have inside? What invention, skills, or deep desire have you left behind, never leaving the ground? What are you waiting to share with the world?

PART 1 REFLECTION

- What makes you happy? Are you allowing the outside world to influence your happiness in any way?
- What lens have you been viewing life through lately? Is your glass half full or half empty?
- Do you feel like you are moving forward, standing still, or moving backward in life? How have you noticed this has impacted your happiness? Explain.
- What or who have you blamed for your dissatisfaction in life? How can you shift this perspective?
- Think about a current or recent problem that has caused you emotional suffering. How can you take a step back and change your perspective to reduce suffering?
- What do you want to attract into your life?
- Think of something you did compulsively recently. How could being conscious of your decision have changed the situation? Brainstorm ways that you will practice consciousness in the future.
- Imagine a situation that is causing you turmoil or dissatisfaction. Graph your current expectations and then brainstorm a more realistic outcome. Identify the gap.

- What external things, appearances, or attitudes do you use to protect your self-esteem/ego? Write three self-affirmations to remind yourself why other people's opinions of you don't matter.
- How can you use your gifts to benefit those around you, your community, and the world?

PART 2

THE LAW OF ATTRACTION (LOA)

Chapter 10

THE LAW OF ATTRACTION

JOY IS THE basis of all things in life. The secret is that you have to be joyful to attract the things you want. When you are joyful, you do things with ease, things come to you easily, doors open for you, and serendipity happens. The universe is on your side when you are in a state of joy. The law that proves this to be true is the Law of Attraction.

Have you ever noticed that friends who hang out together are similar in many ways? That is because like attracts like. This is based on the Law of Attraction (LOA), which states that whatever you think, focus on, and pay attention to is what you will manifest in your life.

Knowing this, you can use the LOA to create the life you want. If you could make all of your wildest dreams come true, what would that look like?

The LOA will get you exponential results instead of incremental results. For example, if you are in sales and you get one lead for every ten calls, you have a ten percent conversion ratio. However, if you apply the LOA, I predict that you could actually make one call and get one lead. That's ten times more effective. Now, don't get me wrong, I don't mean that you should just sit there and meditate on the thought, "I want this sale." The trick is to first "prime" yourself before you do the inspired action.

What is priming yourself? It's when you are in a state of joy or you feel good. When you feel good, you attract good. To use the Law of Attraction to its fullest advantage, follow this process.

Law of Attraction – Process
- Ask
- Given
- Allowing
- Embrace Contrast

Chapter 11

STEP 1: ASK

THE FIRST STEP in the Law of Attraction is to ask.

If you want something, you have to ask for it, forget about the "how," and just work toward it. Everything will start to flow to you and align for you to reach your dreams and goals once you start with this step. The "how" will only stop you from asking. If you don't ask, you won't get it.

For me, my dream is to be a spiritual speaker. In the beginning, this little voice inside of me said, "I want it. I think about it. I dream about it. But I would never tell a soul about it." I was too scared to tell anyone about my dream. I finally started telling my close friends about it, but I was embarrassed because I did not know how to give speeches in public.

At first, I was afraid to do anything with it, but finally, my deep desires overcame my fear. I asked. I started by doing little talks at my house and at a local temple. I read books such as *The Power of Now*, *Happiness Advantage*, *Ask and It's Given*, and more. I wondered, "How come no one knows about this?" and I started sharing what I learned with others. I also joined Toastmasters to practice my public speaking skills, and I became more and more comfortable on stage, even at work. As a Sr. Business Analyst, I present data and analysis to executives, which helps me build my confidence and public speaking skills. At my workplace, I also joined programs to help women become better at public speaking. We used to meet weekly, and I had to write a new speech for every meeting, which led me to become a more confident speaker.

One day, my friend Carlene went to one of my talks. Afterward, she asked me, "Hey, that was a really good talk on this topic. Can you give a talk for our group?"

I replied, "Sure. What is the name of the group, and where is the talk?" It turned out that she wanted me to speak in front of the Taiwanese American Professionals National Convention in Seattle. I had never thought of speaking in front of such a large group—a national convention involving professionals from all over the United States. I was very excited but super nervous. I accepted; however, I did not have any idea of what I was getting myself into.

I was honored to meet so many great people at the convention, and I connected with many people from the conference. A couple of years later, one of the people who had been in the audience asked me how to better manifest her goals using the Law of Attraction. She remembered my talk. I also received emails from other people saying that they wanted to learn more about my topic and what I shared with them at that convention.

So, if I had never declared it to my close friends or talked about what I learned, how in the world would Carlene have known I wanted to do this? Why did I have the opportunity to give a talk at the Taiwanese American Professionals Convention? It happened because I got out of my own way and did it regardless of whether I was scared or not.

You must declare what you want and forget about the "how" because that's not your role. Your responsibility is to work toward your goal, and the universe will open up the doors for you. You will be amazed at the opportunities that present themselves to you.

So, ASK.

It's important to note that there are different ways to ask. You are asking all the time, every day, and every way.

The first way to ask is through our thoughts. This is one of the simplest ways of asking. In the morning, we might think, "I need more energy" or "It would be nice if I didn't have to go to work." When we look in the mirror, we might think, "I need to lose some weight." With all of these thoughts, we are asking for something.

As the saying goes, "Be careful what you wish for, it might come true."

Remember that whatever you think about, you are asking for. What you think about will not instantly come true, but you are asking.

Another ask is to explicitly identify things you want. For example, I saw a movie called *Couples Retreat*, where the characters went to Bora Bora, and I thought, "Wow, that place is so beautiful. I want to go there, too." All these desires can manifest faster or slower, depending on how strongly you feel about them and how quickly you choose to act. I actually went to Bora Bora on my tenth anniversary with my husband and daughter. I wanted to go there since the movie came out in 2009, and I manifested it in 2018! It took nine years for this to come true. So, you never know how long it will take for your wants to come to fruition.

Even more effective than thoughts or wants is what you intentionally focus on. Whatever you focus on expands. For example, if you want to buy a Toyota, you will suddenly start seeing Toyotas everywhere. There were always Toyotas on the road, but because you started focusing on them, you will see more of them. When you learn to focus your energy on what you want, magical things start to happen. Opportunities start showing up for you. Ideas flow to you effortlessly. You meet people who want

Step 1: Ask

to help you or connect you with the right people to help you on your path. You stumble across resources that you needed, or synchronicity starts to occur.

To understand "focus" in a simple way, try this exercise. Close your eyes and remember all the red in the room. Now, open your eyes and look for red in the room. Now, close your eyes, and again, try to remember all the red in the room. Most likely, each time you close your eyes, you will remember more red items in the room. It's because when you deliberately focus on something, you are more conscious of its presence.

When you enter a room, do you scan for positive things or negative things? Do you focus on the dim lights or the beautiful painting? When you go on vacation and it's hot, do you focus on the heat or on the vacation with your family? Whatever you focus on will expand, and you will see more of it. It can be pleasant or unpleasant. What you focus on and how you experience life is your choice.

Once you've decided what you want to focus on, you can make a declaration. Declarations are the strongest type of ask. If I have a BIG want, such as "I want to be a spiritual speaker," then I declare it. I tell the universe that I want it. I tell all my friends about it. I make my desire known—clearly. We make declarations after a clear and conscious choice, unlike thoughts and small wants. Declarations are made with more purpose and stronger desires.

Lastly, I want to caution you about complaining. If you are complaining, that is also asking. If you complain that you don't have any money, you won't have money. If you complain that you do not have a boyfriend, you will not get a boyfriend. If you complain that you are fat, you will be fat. So, stop the complaining.

Some people complain all the time and wonder why their life is a mess. It is because they are always complaining. If they were to talk about the great things in their life, then they would have positive things come into their lives. The universe would reward their positive outlook, and their positive focus would help them notice all the good around them. You can't have a positive life with a negative mind.

Complaining often happens because people don't know what they want. Instead, they look at what they *don't* want. However, by directing your focus this way, you can unintentionally ask for something you don't want. It's a bit of an oxymoron.

For example, if you have a disrespectful, micromanaging boss, you might want a new job with a manager who is nice and respectful and who gives you the freedom to do your job because he trusts you. Instead of saying, "I don't want a mean and disrespectful boss," be affirmative. Say, "I want a nice and respectful boss."

In baseball, people often say, "Don't miss," which actually causes some people to miss the ball because they are now focusing on missing. Avoid saying "don't" ahead of something you want. If you do, then you are asking for the opposite of what you want. Say, "I'm going to make the shot," instead of, "I don't want to miss this shot."

Another example is in relationships. If you are single, you might say, "I don't want someone who is lazy, mean, bald, or a smoker," and you wonder why you attract that type of person. Or you see people who just got out of a relationship, and they say they don't want that kind of relationship anymore with a lying, cheating boyfriend, yet they attract the same type of guy in their next relationship. You attract not only what you do want but what you complain about as well. Everything you see, you either want it or don't want it. Focus on what you want, not what you don't want, and *ask* for it.

Chapter 12

STEP 2: IT IS GIVEN

THE SECOND STEP is *given*. As soon as you ask, the universe will start working to give you what you asked for. That is the job of the universe. You can call on your god, your divine team, your higher power, or whatever you believe. For me, I call Buddha Guan Yin, Ji Gong, Happy Buddha, and the creator—that is my divine team. When I ask, "Hi, Divine Team, can you do or give me this?" they just go and do it.

Imagine that you are the CEO of a company, and you have a right-hand man who does everything for you. When you say that you want a coffee, he goes and gets it for you exactly the way you want it, no questions asked. That is the universe. You can get anything that you want; all you have to do is ask.

Joyful Living

The problem is that most of us ask and wonder if our right-hand man is going to do it. When is he going to do it? How is he going to do it? For example, you ask for a tall, half-decaf, sugar-free hazelnut, soy latte, and you ask your assistant to go get it. After a while, you check on him and ask, "Have you gotten it yet? Did you get my soy latte, not a regular latte? Make sure it is half-decaf, not regular, and not decaf." You follow him and stop him on the road, asking, "Where are you going? Are you going to get my soy latte?" Then, you follow him to Starbucks to make sure he gets the order right. You stop him in front of the Starbucks, demanding he repeat your order to you again. At this point, he will never even make it to the line to order the drink for you. And even if he did, you'd just hound the barista, making sure that they got the order right. Meanwhile, you're still waiting for a drink, and now you're frantic and anxious.

We don't trust the person, or in this case, the universe, to bring what we asked for. We don't trust that the message will be received. We don't trust the process because we don't know exactly how or when we will be given what we asked for. But we have to trust. We have to believe that the universe will understand the ask. We have to trust that the person or entity will understand and get it for us. Our order can't be delivered if we keep doubting it will come or if we are micromanaging the process. We have to get out of the way and let the universe work. Get rid of the questioning and the doubt. Let the universe do its job, and it will deliver on time, exactly how we ordered it. Believe it will come. Sometimes, we even get something better than what we asked for. Say, "Give me this or something better." I want a soy, sugar-free hazelnut latte or something better.

The universe knows what is best for you, so sometimes you will ask for something, and the universe won't get you exactly what you wanted because it's got something even better for you. My dream car was a hardtop Lexus convertible. However, the universe knew I was going to have a baby soon, so it ended up getting me a Lexus SUV. I got something better than what I asked for! The universe knew I needed space for my baby, so it got me an SUV instead.

Remember, it is unnecessary to be stressed about whether or not you will get what you want or need. The universe will deliver if you give it time.

Chapter 13

STEP 3: ALLOW

HAVE YOU EVER wanted something so bad you could feel it? I remember once when I wanted a promotion so badly that I could feel it. I could feel that they would give me the promotion. When you feel it, you can manifest it.

This is a vital step that can help you get what you want; therefore, pay attention to it. The third step in the Law of Attraction is ***allowing***. In this step, you must control your feelings and emotions so you can sync them with the reality you want. Match your feelings to the feelings of the reality that you want, and you cannot help but create that reality.

Essentially, you can feel like you have the car, job, house, vacation, or significant other that you want. Even though you don't have it physically, you can have it vibrationally. Once you can feel it or vibrationally have it, it will come to you. It is on its way to you.

The thing stopping you from receiving is you. In fact, this is the part that stops most of us from getting what we want. We are not allowing our desires to emerge.

The universe responds to your vibrational feelings. The key is to control how you feel when you think about your desires. If you are sad, you are planning for more sadness. Have you ever heard the phrase, "When it rains, it pours"? That phrase is a reflection of this step of the Law of Attraction.

So, stop worrying. It is not going to help you. Instead, be positive and get excited about what the universe has in store for you!

I will give you an example that can help you grasp the idea of this feeling. Suppose you want to listen to 93.3 FM, which is a hip-hop station, but your radio station is dialed into 89.5 FM, which is a trance station. What you want and what you have dialed in are not on the same wavelength. You wonder why you are not hearing the type of music you want. You realize you have to tune your station to 93.3 so that the signal can be sent to the satellite to turn on the station that you want. Similarly, you have to dial into the feeling of your desire, and then you will get what you want. The best way to do this is to assume the feeling even if your wish has yet to materialize.

Pretend that you already have the thing that you want. If you want that new car, go test drive it. Feel it. How does it feel sitting in that Ferrari with the wind blowing your hair? You will feel like you have it already. One of the ways you can practice feeling your goals or dreams is to have a vision board; it actually works. If you visualize it and feel it, then you can manifest it.

If you want something, you need to feel it. If you are broke, do you feel like you are broke, or do you feel like you have an abundance of money? If you say you want more money, but you feel you lack money, you will not be able to manifest it. You see how you can fail to dial in. If you want 93.3, but you are feeling 89.5, then you will not get it.

You also have to believe it to manifest it. Napoleon Hill has a famous quote: "Whatever the mind can conceive and believe, it can achieve!"[1] So, whatever you want, you have to believe it. You can do all these affirmations and vision boards, but if you don't believe it, you can't manifest it.

Let Your Emotions Guide You

What you feel, you attract. So, you can use your emotions as your guidance system. At any time of the day, you can gauge where your emotions are at. If you are not feeling well emotionally, then you know that you have to work on your feelings.

Here is an emotional guidance scale so you can identify your vibrational level. In this scale, love is the highest

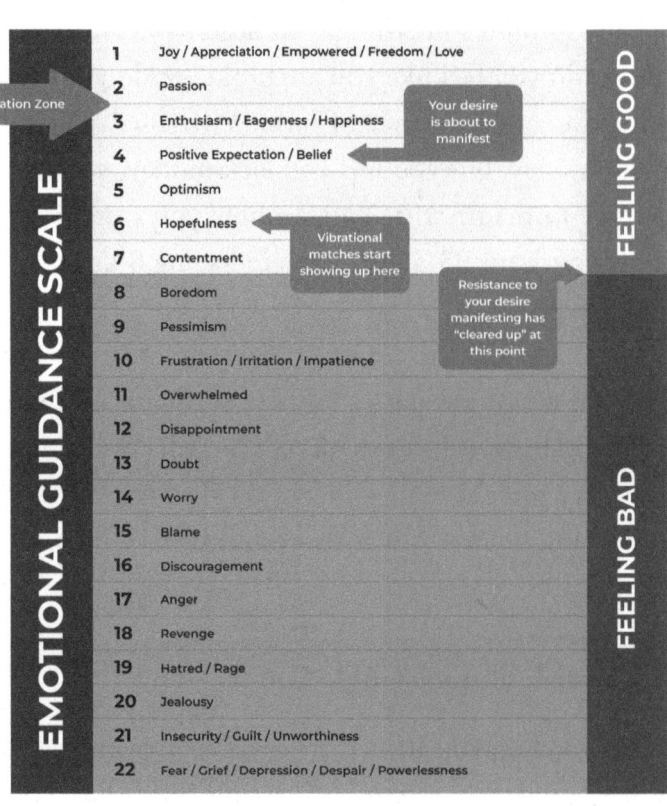

vibration, and depression is the lowest vibration. Love is when you see your child smile, your dog is pleased to see you, or you spend time with your partner. Depression is when you feel like life does not have anything to offer you. That is the worst feeling, which is why it is ranked the lowest.

Using this scale, you can identify how you're feeling, and then you can figure out if you are moving up or down the scale. If you feel worried and you move up the scale to doubt, you are moving in a positive direction. If you feel anger and you want revenge, and then you move to hatred and jealousy, then you know that you are moving in a negative direction.

The Momentum of Thoughts

Feelings start with a thought, and then that thought picks up momentum. Have you ever thought of something, an argument perhaps, and then started getting angry at that person, and then, as you continued to think about it, you spiraled from anger to rage to resentment? Well, that happened because there is momentum in your thoughts, and thoughts turn into feelings.

It's similar to a car going down a hill. It picks up speed as it moves downward. Thus, it is difficult to make a hard stop at the bottom of the hill. So, how do you stop it from picking up too much speed? The best thing you can do is stop the downhill momentum at the top of the hill before it picks up speed to begin with.

For example, if you were on top of the hill with your car in neutral, and then you nudged it forward slowly, and just as it starts to roll downhill, you hit the brakes, then the car would stop quickly. But if you were to nudge it forward and let it roll all the way to the bottom, do you think you could stop it as easily there? Probably not.

The same applies to thoughts and emotions. If you have a negative thought, you can catch it and stop it before it fuels negative emotions. So, be careful what you think about. Once you start to pay attention and be mindful of what you think about, you can stop any negative momentum.

However, if you are thinking about something and start getting excited about it, then let it build. You will create momentum to build on those positive aspects. When you are in a good mood, you attract positive things in your life.

Your thoughts create your emotions, and your emotions attract what you feel. If you feel good, you attract good. Have you ever had a great day, and suddenly, you're running into all the green lights, and you have the front-row parking space wherever you go? Then, at Starbucks, they make your drink perfectly, and when you get to work, all your co-workers are working together peacefully on a project you enjoy. Days like these are the result of your good mood and positive demeanor at the start of the day. Everything is going smoothly because you are in a good mood.

But what if you're not in a good mood? You go get coffee, and it spills all over you. When you get to work, all the parking spaces are taken, and you have to park far away. And when you get inside, your co-workers didn't finish their side of the project. What the heck? When it rains, it pours. This bad momentum is the result of your bad mood.

Your thoughts magnify your emotions, and due to the LOA, you attract what you feel. If you feel good, you attract good things. If you feel bad, you attract bad things in your life.

So, if you notice your negative thoughts, stop them before they turn into emotions. If you are complaining, stop complaining. Focus on the positive aspects of the person or situation, and more positive aspects of that person or situation will come to fruition. Change the negative words into positive words and the negative emotions into positive ones. That is how you can attract the positive aspects of the things you want.

Master the Art of Allowing

Once you can manage your thoughts and feelings, you will be able to master the art of allowing. You will be able to master your own vibrations and emotions. When you are off-track, you will be able to get back on track right away. You master the allowing mode.

You are in the zone, and your life is good. When you are driving, the green lights are on. When you arrive at

Joyful Living

the mall, you get front-row parking. Why? It is because you are in the zone. Have you ever heard someone say, "He is in the zone. He is making deals happen left and right?" It's because he's feeling good all the time.

When you feel good, everything seems good, and you are ready to receive good things from the universe. You have mojo, and everything is aligning for you. Whenever you have a desire, you manifest it faster because you mastered allowing. You are in the receiving mode. Life is sweet for you.

Chapter 14

STEP 4: EMBRACE CONTRAST

THE FOURTH AND final step in the Law of Attraction is to *embrace contrast*. Contrast refers to the problems, obstacles, and adversities you deal with throughout your life. Once you have awareness, you can say to yourself, "Oh, I know this is contrast. I know what is happening." Then, you can embrace contrast and adversity instead of getting upset or annoyed.

Everything happens to you for a reason. You should learn from obstacles in your life so that you do not make the same mistakes again. Contrast helps you expand your desires and grow as a person.

Think of contrast as something that will help you learn and grow. You have to go through it. Once you get to the other side, you are going to be way better than you were before.

When you hit adversity, you have three choices: accept it, change your desire, or do something about it.

I remember when I wanted to switch careers and try to apply for a new position. I really wanted it, which was the ask, but I didn't think I was good enough, and I did not do the allowing step. I still applied for the position and got the job interview, but I didn't get the job. I was very disappointed. This was contrast. I could either accept it and just stay at my job, try another position, or learn from this experience and try again. I chose the latter. I remembered all the interview questions they asked me, and I practiced and prepared for the next opportunity. It helped me grow to be more confident and gave me knowledge of the position. When the opportunity was available, I was ready and applied for the position again. This time, I was more confident, and I believed I could get the job! Having confidence and believing in yourself is allowing. And lo and behold, I got the job!

Another contrast was the COVID-19 pandemic. It caused everyone to panic and become scared for their life. People didn't want to go out. Corporations made everyone work from home. First, it was scary, and then people started adjusting. Working from home actually helped people get more of their time back instead of commuting to work. They had more energy to work because they didn't have to be stuck in traffic. Corporations saved more money on office spaces, and people saved money by not paying for gas to go to work. At first, it was a huge contrast, but now, everyone likes working from home. If you are sick, you can still Zoom into meetings or work from home. Now, it's a new way of doing business. Our temple used to go to the temple every week for class, but now, after the pandemic, we still use Zoom because it's convenient for us, and more people from across the country or world can Zoom into class. It has expanded across the country and across borders!

When you experience contrast, remember that the universe is there to help you grow and expand. Once you have this perspective, you will not feel as much pain and suffering because you will embrace the contrast.

**My Manifestation
and How I Embrace Contrast**

I want to share with you my manifestation after I learned about the Law of Attraction. It actually helped my life exponentially. I am the type of person who, if I want something, I go get it. If I want a job, I will work hard for it and get it. If I want to lose weight, I work on it and lose the pounds I need to get there. But there was one thing I really wanted but couldn't get, and that was having kids. My dream was to have a family and raise them in a good neighborhood. When my husband and I were trying, it was tough because I had complications, and we had to use intervention. We tried for a couple of years, but it didn't happen. It was the lowest point in my life. I didn't know what to live for anymore. I didn't know what would make me happy. Even though my husband knew I wanted to have kids, he didn't know how much it shattered me and how disappointed I was. I remember I was working, and the nurse called and told me the negative news. I almost broke down and cried right there. I couldn't work. I took a walk outside to just get some fresh air. It was fall, and I looked at the leaves turning and wondered what life was all about.

After a few months, I found an online course called Destiny by Design.[1] That is when I discovered the Law of Attraction. The course taught me that I could manifest whatever I wanted. I thought, "Wow, let me see if I can manifest a child." I took the course and started applying it in my life. I used this law to manifest my first daughter. When I was introduced to this process, I dedicated myself to it, and within a few months, we were able to conceive.

I manifested my first daughter when I was on vacation. After we came back from vacation, I found out that I was pregnant. During that vacation mode—allowing mode, receptive mode, or simply feeling good—everything just kept coming to me at one thousand miles per hour; everything I wanted came to fruition. When you are on vacation, you are in allowing mode, and things just come to you without you even asking. That's called a miracle alert! The best time to ask is when you are in vacation mode. You don't have to be on an actual vacation; you can imagine you are on vacation and be in vacation mode. You can create your own vacation in your backyard or retreat in your own home.

When we tried for our second child, we got twins! It was definitely a "or something better" result. I call it the double miracle! If you allow the universe to help you and you believe that you will get what you want, the miracle will happen. I got my miracles!

When the kids arrived, we started having exponential results in business as well. I don't know if it was because they brought so much joy to us or not, but it was working. I continued to prime myself every morning and be positive as much as possible.

My next dream was to buy a modern home in a good neighborhood. In the end, we bought a home that was double our budget and located near the best schools in the state! I remember after meditating one day, I thought, "Wouldn't it be nice to live in this very desired neighborhood? It's close to downtown and the beach, and it has all the amenities I ever wanted." We ended up buying in that neighborhood. These are just a few things I manifested after applying all these practices. It's not going to happen overnight, but I would say my life is exponentially better than I ever dreamed it would be. Now, I am just trying to give back and share what I learned so others can benefit from it as well.

When I discovered the Law of Attraction, I worked on myself every morning to be in a state of peace and joy. Throughout the day, I try to notice my thoughts more and redirect them to where I want to go rather than what I don't want. In life, we can complain and notice all the bad things in the world, or we can notice all the good in the world. Be happy not because everything is good but because you see the good in everything.

Everything just started coming into place for me when I started practicing this Law of Attraction. I appreciated the things I wanted instead of complaining about the things I didn't want. When you appreciate what you have, the universe will give you more of it. If you don't, it will take it away.

When I was young, I always looked for the good side of things. I remember when I was working in the corporate world, and we had a huge layoff. They laid off thirty percent of the workforce. It was a brutal day for everyone. We were safe, and I said to my colleagues, "At least we are safe."

They replied, "Liên, life is not all rose-colored glasses. You never know when you will be next." I knew that, but at least I appreciated where I was and that I still had a job. I didn't know it then, but I know now that my lens of the world has always been positive. I always try to make the most of everything. The co-workers I knew who got let go were the ones who complained a lot about the job and gossiped. It's really true when people say,

"Appreciate what you have, or it will be taken from you." So, appreciate your job if you still have it, or your spouse, your kids, or your health. And the most important thing to appreciate is that you are still alive. Without your life, you can't do all or have all the things you want.

The key to the Law of Attraction is to focus on the things you want instead of the things you don't want. Sync up to the feelings of the thing you want. Be mindful of your thoughts and emotions and act accordingly. Embrace whatever life throws at you. There's always a reason why things happen, and it's always happening for you, not to you. Maybe it's helping you expand and grow from where you are at. Keep doing the best you can with the capacity you have, and be positive. Have faith, and believe everything will work out for you. If you do that, you will be able to be, do, and have anything you want.

Chapter 15

SUMMARY OF LOA

YOU WERE MEANT to have a happy life. You were meant to live out your dreams. Declare what you want, focus on it, pay attention to how you feel, and embrace adversity. Then, take inspired action and watch the miracles happen!

I am not telling you to say, "I want this" or "I want that," and sit on the couch and watch TV all day and meditate. No! You have to take inspired action. If I want to go to Bora Bora for my wedding anniversary, I have to do the research and call the travel agent to book the ticket. I have to research, look into the trip, and make the call. By doing these things, I will make this trip happen by taking inspired action. When you want something, and you take action toward it, the universe will open doors for you. Everything will start aligning, and you will wonder how it was even possible.

I never thought in a million years that I would get the life that I have right now, with a loving family, a wonderful career, and a life filled with so much joy. I look at the great things that I have in my life, and I keep getting more of them.

As my mentor Thach Nguyen said, "Appreciate what you have and be eager for more. The more you appreciate, the more the universe gives to you. Be a deliberate creator of the life that you want and enjoy the ride."

Your goal is to feel joy. Do what makes your heart sing. Once you do, everything will fall into place; everything you want will come to fruition even faster. The Law of Attraction works exponentially, so be mindful of what you feel and focus on.

PART 2 REFLECTION

- What dreams do you want to achieve using the Law of Attraction?
- What do you need to *ask* to achieve your dreams? What thoughts do you need to stop?
- What is stopping you from believing that the universe can and will do what you ask?
- How have you previously viewed contrast in your life? What daily obstacles do you face, and how can you embrace them?
- What inspired action(s) do you need to take to achieve your goals?

PART 3

HAPPINESS HABITS

HAPPINESS HABITS ARE where the rubber meets the road. Practicing these habits is how you can exponentially increase your happiness. Being joyful sounds simple, but it's not easy to do, so you have to practice it daily, like lifting weights. You get stronger over time. Yes, life is going to hit you with things that make you unhappy, but with practice, you can raise your baseline happiness and get back where you left off more easily. It's like the shock absorbers in your car; when you hit a bumpy road, it doesn't hit you that hard because they absorb the shock. If someone says something that upsets you, instead of being upset for a month, it might take you a week to get over it. And over time, negativity will not affect you as much, and you will move on in a day or even just seconds. With these daily practices and habits, you can be happier and reach your highest potential.

Chapter 16

MIRACLE MORNING

ONE TIME, WHEN I was at a workshop, a woman shared a book called *Miracle Morning* by Hal Elrod with me. When I first saw it, I thought, "I'm not a morning person. But I'll read it just to see what it's about." However, when I started reading it, I felt as if the book was about me.

The book prompted an important question: Are you waking up pushing the snooze button? I thought, "Yeah, I push it every day." Then, Elrod argued that if the answer is yes, you are pushing the snooze button on your life. I read the first few chapters, and I was inspired.

Elrod asks questions and stirs thoughts, such as, what if you woke up every day and it felt like Christmas? Do you remember when you were a kid, and you couldn't wait to open your presents? Isn't it more exciting to wake up to that feeling than "Oh no, I have to wake up and go to work, take care of the kids, and run errands?" It struck a chord in me. I said to myself, "I don't want to wake up and just force myself to get through the day."

Elrod wrote, "The last thing you thought of will be the first thing you think about the next morning."[1] I was inspired to wake up without pushing the snooze button. I was determined to change my life and wake up differently.

So, I tried what he suggested. Before I went to sleep, I thought of how excited I was to start my Miracle Morning as if it were Christmas the next day! I usually woke up at 8 a.m., but this time, I set the alarm one hour early so I could start my day before everyone else woke up. He advised readers to put their alarm clocks across the bedroom or somewhere far away from their bed, so they have to get up. Then, go to the bathroom, drink a glass of water, brush your teeth, or put on your gym clothes. But don't hit the snooze button. So, I got my gym clothes ready with my tennis shoes. I put the alarm far away. When the alarm went off, I didn't push the snooze button. I got excited to start my day like it was Christmas. I got up, put on my tennis shoes, and went outside to take a walk. I noticed all the flowers in my neighborhood and a butterfly fluttering by me, which landed on one of the flowers. The air was crisp because it was early morning, and there were no cars yet. It was only me walking along my neighborhood street. I thought, "Wow, it's nice to have alone time before my day starts."

If you haven't tried it yet, you'll be amazed at how much you get done and how much happier it makes you to start your day on the right track.

Hal Erold discovered Miracle Morning after hitting rock bottom. He wanted to be successful and started researching common themes among successful people. He found that successful people do one or all of what he called "SAVERS," which stands for "Silence, Affirmations, Visualize, Exercise, Read, and Scribing."[2] He explained, "Your level of success can never exceed your level of personal development. Who you think you are on the inside—including your belief, perspective, and attitude—decides how you think and act, and thus the results you achieve."[3] Elrod shares how he used the Miracle Morning to bounce back from his near-death experience, crippling injuries, and career setback to then unlock his full potential. Elrod described six SAVERS steps in *Miracle Morning*:

> **Silence:** Start your day in silence. Meditate, take a few deep breaths, quiet the mind, and block out the chatter. Have a calm, peaceful, and centered mind.
>
> **Affirmation:** Words of encouragement are powerful because they help you get motivated to go after your dreams or goals, overcome your fears, be healthy and happy, and live out your purpose.

Visualization: Whatever you can imagine, you can manifest. Visualize yourself doing the steps you need to accomplish your goals, and then imagine how you would feel if you were doing them.

Exercise: Get your body moving so blood and oxygen flow to your brain. Even five minutes will help get your circulation going. It will wake up your body and brain to do what you need to do for the day.

Reading: Fill your brain with positive thoughts, knowledge, and ideas to improve yourself and accomplish your daily tasks.

Scribing: Journaling or writing is a great way to process your thoughts and reflect on your life. Putting your feelings on paper will help you be more self-aware and articulate.[4]

Many people dream of an extraordinary life but end up with a mediocre one. No matter where you are in life, whether you are overcoming a major setback or ready to move to new heights, be happier, and more successful, the Miracle Morning will help you improve all aspects of your life.

Life is precious, and when you wake up in the morning, it's a miracle! You are still alive. We should celebrate it every day and cherish the time we have here. By starting the day early and doing the SAVERS steps, we can start the day refreshed, excited, and content.

It's important to note that you don't *have* to do all the SAVERS; you can choose the ones that make your day better. The point of SAVERS is not to force you to waste your time on unhelpful tasks, but instead, it is meant to give you plenty of options to choose from to create a peaceful morning of your design. I do MAIDE. I Meditate, write my AID (Appreciation, Intention, and Delegate), and Exercise. I will share more about AID in the next chapter.

When I do my morning routine, everything flows, but when I don't, for some reason, my day is off. I try my best to do my MAIDE every morning. If I can't do all of it, I meditate. It's the one thing I must do every day. It helps me be centered, grounded, and at peace. With my busy schedule of bouncing between picking up my kids, working, and volunteering, I need to be at my best, and that starts with silence or meditation.

A happy, fulfilling life is within your reach. Take purposeful action and do what is best for you in the morning. By starting your day off right, you will give yourself the momentum to conquer your day with a peaceful mind, thus providing you with the happiness and fulfillment you deserve all day long. Due to your habitual, intentional, and visionary practices, everything will start aligning for you. Your dreams will come true over time as you work toward them.

Chapter 17

AID (APPRECIATION, INTENTION, DELEGATION)

ONE OF THE first things I do in the morning is write down my AID: Appreciation, Intention, and Delegation. I learned this from the Destiny by Design course I mentioned previously. I start the morning in a positive way by setting myself up for a good mood. For appreciation, I write, "Today I appreciate . . ." and then I write all the things I appreciate. I appreciate the things I have, and I don't think about what I don't have. I focus on the fact that I do have a job, I can pay my bills, I have a car, and I have a house that keeps me warm. When gratitude becomes essential to the foundation of our lives, miracles start to appear everywhere.

Then, I write my intentions. "Today I am committed to being and feeling . . ." Every day, I write what I

Joyful Living

want to be that day. Most of the time, my focus is to be vibrant, courageous, conscious, healthy, and joyful. We live in a world of doing, but we need to work on *being*. If we determine who we want to be, the doing will follow. Happiness is not an event; it's a state of being.

Last but not least, I delegate to the universe what I want for the day, week, year, or for my life. I state: "Thank you in advance, divine team, for assisting me with . . ." You can choose anyone in your divine team: God, Jesus, your ancestors, such as your mom, your dad, your grandma, your grandpa, or anyone in your circle. I ask my divine team for what I want, and then I trust the universe or my divine team to help me get it. Remember, the first step in the Law of Attraction is to ask for what you want. Ask for anything and everything you want. The universe or your divine team will orchestrate it for you. Whatever the result is, it will come as you hoped or as something even better than what you asked for.

Here is an example of my AID:

- **Appreciation:** Today, I appreciate that I had a good night's sleep, I am alive, my family is alive, I had a productive day yesterday, and I am blessed with a beautiful home, kids, and life.
- **Intention:** Today, I am committed to being and feeling courageous, conscious, healthy, and joyful.
- **Delegate:** Thank you in advance, Divine Team, for assisting me with a good night's sleep, keeping my family and me healthy, helping me finish writing my bestselling

book, helping my kids do well in school, and growing our business. Also, thank you in advance for a great weekend with my family. Thanks, Divine Team, for orchestrating this for me.

Appreciation

Now that we've discussed AID, I want to reiterate the importance of the appreciation aspect because it will make all the difference in the outcome of your day, week, and life. One of the best ways to stay positive is to practice appreciation. When you look at the positive aspects of a situation, it shifts your energy.

You can't control what happens around you, but you can control your state of being. You can manage your expectations and choose to be grateful for all that you have instead of dwelling on less-than-ideal circumstances outside of your control.

When gratitude becomes an essential foundation in your life, miracles will start to appear everywhere. The more you appreciate, the more the universe will give you. When you focus on what you don't have, you are telling the universe that you don't appreciate what has been given to you. So, the universe will take things away from you. For example, if you say, "I hate my job" or "I hate my boss," you will go to work unhappy. People can feel your energy. You repel people when you are grumpy. So, when the company has a layoff, guess who will be the first to go? Assuming that everyone has the same skillset, the people who complain and are unhappy will most likely be let go first. So, appreciate what you have, or you will not have it anymore.

If you appreciate your job and your coworkers, they will want to work with you. If you show your appreciation to your boss and value the job and the opportunities it gives you, they will support you in your job and help you with your career. Appreciate what you have, and be eager for more! Likewise, always concentrate on how far you've come rather than how far you have left to go. People often look at how far they have to go to reach their goals instead of how far they have come. They feel overwhelmed or dissatisfied. But often, when they look back at how far they have come, they realize they have actually accomplished a lot.

When I look at my life, I think about how far I've come in my goal to be a spiritual speaker. I overcame my fear of public speaking and have influenced many people to be positive and reach their goals. I have been working on myself for the past few years, and I am finally writing this book! It took longer than I thought it would, but I am happy about my progress as long as I am improving every day. I paused from writing this book because I had my double-miracle twins! So, the pause was actually a blessing. My children bring so much joy to my life.

I've chosen to look forward instead of back. I trust that the universe will help me. I'm doing the activities I need to do in order to get where I want to go, and I'm enjoying the process. I'll leave the results up to the divine.

Practice Appreciating the Little Things

Life is short, so do things that make you happy. Enjoy the little moments with your kids, the joy of being able to dance, and your ability to be present with your loved ones. Life can be tough sometimes, but we have to practice joy in the midst of the storm. The storm will pass because it was there for a reason: for you to grow and learn. So, don't be scared. Does ignoring the storm and embracing appreciation sound difficult? Don't know where to start? Here are a few ideas of ways to practice appreciation:

- Start by smiling and saying, "I am thankful to be alive today," and then smile again, saying, "I'm thankful my family is alive."
- Thank your body for functioning, even if your body isn't ideal. Look after your body and embrace how amazing it is. Move and nourish it with fresh food.
- Think about and be thankful for the roof over your head, the food on your table, and your warm clothes.
- Be thankful that you have a job, regardless of whether it is an ideal situation or not. Many people don't have a job.

- Appreciate meaningful experiences and focus less on material possessions.
- Be thankful for nature. Go to the woods or on a hike. Find somewhere beautiful you've never been before and appreciate all that is around you.
- Take a walk in your neighborhood. Notice the fresh air, the bird song, and the beautiful scenery.
- Listen to music with focus. Take in the lyrics and melodies and different instruments. Let it be therapy, and appreciate its meaning.
- Cuddle your dog or cat. Be thankful for their comfort and love.
- Talk to your friends in person. Feel their love and support and offer it in return. Be grateful for them, and show them you appreciate them.
- Tell your loved ones you love them every time you get the chance, and love them with everything you have. Always remember how grateful you are to have them in your life.
- Give, give, give. You gain more happiness doing things for others than doing them for yourself. Be thankful for the resources you can share with others.

You have a conscious choice to make: complain about or appreciate the situation you're in. Think about how drastically your energy would shift if you simply redirected your thoughts toward the positive. Choose happiness deliberately. Don't leave it to chance. Decide upon waking what kind of day you'll have. Focus on higher thoughts, energies, vibrations, and experiences.

I encourage you to try to appreciate and love every little thing you can, then watch as this transforms your mindset and your life!

Chapter 18

MEDITATION AND MINDFULNESS

SCIENTIFIC STUDIES SHOW that meditation can help to reduce stress, lower blood pressure, improve sleep quality, improve focus, extend memory, increase creativity, strengthen the immune system, improve relationships, and increase happiness. Meditation rewires your brain for happiness, peace, and success.[1]

Meditation helps you slow down and lets your mind rest. You can do simple meditation by taking deep breaths for fifteen minutes and concentrating on your breathing, or you can listen to a guided meditation. You can find one online or download an app to help with guided meditation. I like Sattva, Calm, or Abraham Hick's fifteen-minute meditations. Deepak Chopra and Oprah also have guided meditations to help you improve your life in areas like health, relationships, or grace.

Your brain is like a snow globe. When you think a thought, it keeps shaking around, and you can't really focus on anything because of the snowstorm going on. But when you stop shaking it and put it down, over time, the snow will fall to the ground, and you can clearly see what's inside the globe.

When you meditate, your brain is calm. You can clearly see what your goals are and what direction you want to go in. Although it's not easy to meditate and be calm, through practice and discipline, you can achieve peace and happiness over time. Your body and mind will thank you.

Mindful Health

Stress is one of the biggest causes of disease. That's why it's called dis-*ease*, because you are not at ease. It weakens your immune system, so you can't fight diseases as effectively. When you are not stressed, your body can fight off those diseases more easily.

Dr. Ellen Langer, a professor at Harvard University and author of many mindfulness books, explained that small instances of mindless behavior tie us to the past. Mindlessness blocks the possibility of being alive in the moment and keeps us from being alert to possibilities. Langer calls her pursuit of mindfulness "The Psychology of Possibility."[2]

Essentially, Langer's definition of mindfulness is "the process of actively noticing new things, relinquishing preconceived mindsets, and then acting on new observations."[3] The goal is to create a healing lifestyle.

Langer notices that most of our behavior is mindless. By becoming more aware of our thoughts, ideas, emotions, and the actions that follow, we will see how they are impacting our bodies in real time. Then, our lives can be transformed at every level.

The mind is quite powerful. It can help you or hurt you. You have to be mindful of what you think and do. Before you do anything or make a decision, pause for a moment and think about *why* you are doing what you're doing. Over time, you will be living more mindfully and not blaming anyone else for how your life unfolds. You can direct it any way you want, like toward improving your health, happiness, peace, and well-being. You can change your life if you are mindful about practicing positive thoughts and actions.

In his book *The Healing Self*, Dr. Deepak Chopra recapped a study on how the mind can heal the body. He explained that the mind and body are one. If you look at these things as one, then you can heal your body.[4] For example, if you want to lose weight, you might work really hard at losing weight, but then after you lose a few pounds, you go back to your habit of overeating. The underlying problem with weight loss is not the weight; it's the separation of the body and mind.

We struggle with what the mind wants to achieve and what the body is actually doing. The separation of the mind from the body is the core of the problem. We would benefit greatly if we would just be mindful of what our body needs and align our thoughts with those needs. For example, "I am hungry, so I will eat," or "I am full, so I will stop eating." We tend to overeat because of boredom, cravings, or because we want comfort. If we pay attention to why we are eating, many of us can solve our weight loss problems effortlessly.

When we look at our body and mind as one, we return to our natural state of well-being. If we are conscious of what we do, we will enjoy being alive and awake. Our whole system becomes more normalized, and this will pay off in dividends.

Present in the Moment

Being present in the moment is a critical aspect of mindfulness. We often hear people say, "Be present, be present," but what does this really mean? Being present involves the intentional, conscious practice of not dwelling on the past and not dreading the future, but instead, focusing wholly on your experience in the present moment.

If we are living in the past, we're thinking about something that does not exist anymore. Why torture ourselves thinking about the past when we can't really control it? Just let it go. And the future is not here yet, so why worry about it? Every moment is a new moment. Be aware and alert and be present in the moment.

Often, our minds wander to things that are beyond our control, whether it be past mistakes or uncertainties in the future. These thoughts wreak havoc on our emotions and productivity. The longer we dwell on these worries, the less time we spend being productive and, therefore, successful. Additionally, when we repeatedly think about the past or worry about the future, we create negative cyclical thought patterns, or habits, and we find that it gets harder and harder to focus on the present and be happy with our current situation.

Obviously, we all must reference and learn from the past and plan intelligently for the future, but we should not live there. We need to live *now*, in the present. Otherwise, we will not be living in reality. Engage your senses and appreciate all that is around you; do this as often as possible. We have the opportunity *now* to make a difference in our lives. We can only positively influence our future by focusing on our present.

Psychological Time

Our minds are always thinking in terms of time, either the past, present, or future. When discussing being present in the moment, it's important to define the different types of "time" we are living in. There are two kinds of time: clock time and psychological time. Clock time helps you plan and make appointments. You use this time to honor your progress for your goals or plans. Psychological time is the time you spend dwelling on the past and feeling angry about things that have happened to you. Psychological time is also when you are feeling anxious about the future. Your mind churns as you think about how to pay a bill or how to finish a project.

As humans, if something has happened in our past, such as abuse, we will remember it for days, weeks, or even years. We may accumulate fear for forty years or for the rest of our lives. We might be afraid to trust anyone, or we might live in fear when we go out alone. We become paralyzed and unable to use our minds to learn from the past or plan for the future. We let the past hinder our potential and keep us from being ourselves.

To be clear, it's okay to pay a brief visit to the past when you need it for a practical reason. But try to be in the present moment most of the time and see how your life changes for the better. The present moment is all you have.

Practice being in the now. If you are in the shower, be in the shower. Notice the water hitting your skin, your breath, and the temperature. It will help you practice being present in your body in the moment. You'll know you're successful at this by the degree of peace you feel within.

Trust that your mind is an instrument, a tool you can use when you need it. Our life purpose is to enjoy the present, accept who we are, appreciate all that there is, and be present in the now. There is never a time when our life is not "this moment."

Chapter 19

USE YOUR BRAIN'S RESOURCES WELL

OUR BRAIN'S RESOURCES are limited. So, we're left with a choice: to use our finite resources to see only pain, negativity, stress, and uncertainty, or to use those resources to look at things through a lens of gratitude, hope, resilience, optimism, and meaning. We can use our brains to change how we process the world. In turn, that changes how we react to the world.

Happiness is not about lying to ourselves or turning a blind eye to the negative. It's about adjusting our brains to rise above our circumstances.

For example, maybe you receive the devastating news that you are being laid off, but you will receive a good severance package. Thinking long-term, you make the decision to use that money to invest in a business. A year later, all your previous colleagues get laid off, too. At first, you feel a little resentful that they were able to keep their jobs for an extra year. Then you find out that because economic circumstances have changed, your colleagues are not going to get severance pay. So, in hindsight, you were better off being laid off earlier.

When something bad happens to you, instead of thinking that it's a bad thing, see it as a temporary setback that might help you in your life. Don't let the outside world affect your inner world. No matter what happens in the outside world, it shouldn't change who you are and your happiness.

By changing our perspectives on what happens to us, we can change the results of our lives. In other words, "reality" is merely our brain's relative understanding of the world based on where and how we are observing it. Most importantly, we can change this perspective at any moment and, by doing so, change our experience of the world around us. Essentially, our mindset and, in turn, our experience of the world, is never set in stone. It is constantly in flux.

While reading the book *The Happiness Advantage*, I learned a great quote from the famous scientist Archimedes, who said, "Give me a lever long enough and a fulcrum on which to place it, and I shall move the world!"[1]

For example, imagine a large boy and a small boy sitting on either side of a seesaw. If you move the fulcrum toward the bigger boy, the lighter boy will seemingly weigh more than the heavier boy. With a single finger, the lighter boy can now use the seesaw lever to move his heavier friend up. In other words, by shifting the point around which energy is applied, we can effectively turn the seesaw from a balancing scale into a powerful lever and then, as Archimedes said, move the world.

Our brains work in precisely the same way. Our power to maximize our potential is based on two important things:

- The length of our lever – how much potential power and possibility we believe we have
- The position of the fulcrum – the mindset with which we generate the power to change

Basically, this means that whether you are a student trying to get better grades, an entrepreneur striving to be successful in business, or an inspirational speaker wanting to impact the world, you don't need to try so hard to produce results. Our potential is not fixed. The more we move our fulcrum, or mindset, the longer our lever grows and the more power we generate. If we move the fulcrum to a positive mindset, then the lever's power is magnified and ready to move everything up. However, if we move the fulcrum to a negative mindset, we will never rise above the ground. You can't have a positive life with a negative mindset.

Our external "reality" is far more malleable than many of us think, and it is far more dependent on how we view it. With the right mindset, our power to dictate this reality increases exponentially.

Chapter 20

JOB, CAREER, OR CALLING

FOR MANY OF us, our jobs take up a considerable amount of time. So, how do we focus on being present and applying the principles from this book to our work lives?

I appreciate psychologist Amy Wrzesniewski's view on this topic. She found that employees have one of three "work orientations," or mindsets about work: job, career, or calling.

She explains that people with a "job" see work as a chore and their paycheck as the reward. They work because they have to and constantly look forward to the time they can spend away from their job. In contrast, people who view their work as a career work not only out of necessity but also to advance and succeed. They are invested in their work and want to do well. Finally, people with a calling view work as fulfilling, not because of external rewards, but because they feel it contributes to the greater good, draws on their personal strengths, and gives them meaning and purpose. Unsurprisingly, people with a calling orientation find their work more rewarding but also work harder and longer because of it. As a result, these are the people who are generally more likely to get ahead.[1]

You might be wondering, "What if I am not working at a job I like or it's not my calling?" It doesn't matter *what* you are doing; it's about your mindset. One can work as a janitor and see their work as a contribution to the cleanliness of the classrooms, which, therefore, helps enhance students' learning and gives them a better future. Another janitor can see their job as just a way to pay the bills. Likewise, one doctor might see his job as stressful work, while another sees it as work that improves people's health and well-being. They both do the same tasks every day, but their different mindsets dictate their work satisfaction, their sense of fulfillment, and, ultimately, how well they do their job.

In his book *The Happiness Advantage*, Shawn Achor encourages individuals to rewrite their job descriptions to "calling descriptions" to highlight the meaning of their work and how their tasks connect to a larger purpose.[2] The more we can align our personal vision with our daily tasks, the more likely we are to see work as a calling.

When you wake up, you have a fresh new start. You can choose a different thought pattern. You have the power to choose what you think and how you feel, and therefore, you can choose to be more present and believe that you have a great purpose in your work and in your life, even if your present situation isn't your end goal. Don't wait to be happy. Find joy and purpose in what you do now.

Chapter 21

BRING YOUR ENERGY UP

FOR THOSE DAYS when you don't feel upbeat or positive, there are many things you can do to get your energy back up. I will share a few strategies with you here.

In a newsletter by Guru Sri Sri Ravi Shankar, I read about how he transforms lower energy into higher energy. He is a humanitarian, spiritual leader, and an ambassador of peace. He is also the founder of the Art of Living Foundation, which promotes yoga, meditation, and powerful breathing techniques.

Shankar implied that since our death can happen at any moment, the very remembrance of our mortality can transform our lower energy into higher energy. By remembering your mortality, you will be motivated to do what is important to you instead of doing nonsense stuff that doesn't matter. You will work on your life goals and spend time with people who are important in your life. You will not spend time gossiping or doing mundane things that don't matter in your life. When you shift to focusing on high-priority things, your life will be enhanced tremendously by feelings of productivity and accomplishment. You will feel fulfilled because of all the important things you have been able to do.

Steve Jobs said, "If you live each day as if it were your last, someday you'll be right. Every morning, I look in the mirror and ask myself, if today were the last day of my life, would I want to do what I do today?" When you change your mindset to live each day as your last, you are reminded of how precious life is and appreciate being alive. You don't take life for granted and your energy shifts to being blissful, grateful, and motivated to make the most of everything.

If you don't feel like you can make that mindset shift yet, you can work on your physical body instead. Personally, when my energy is low, I do Qi Gong, an ancient Chinese exercise, to wake up my body and mind. I encourage you to give it a try. Here are the steps:

1. The first step is to stand with your feet shoulder-width apart. Lift one leg and use both of your hands to tap both sides of your ankle. Then, slowly tap to your knee, then your thigh. Repeat on the other ankle, knee, and thigh.

Bring Your Energy Up

2. Bend slightly forward with a straight back and tap your lower back for a minute.
3. Lift one hand straight out in front of you. Use your other hand to tap under your armpit. Then, tap the top of your hand and slowly tap toward your shoulder. Do the same for the other side.
4. Choose three words that represent what you want to be. Tap the top of your head, repeating those three words with each tap. Then, tap the back of your head and repeat those three words. Then, with both your right and left hands, tap on both sides of your head, repeating those three words. Finally, tap the top of your forehead, cheek, and chin while repeating those three words.
5. Let your hands dangle to your right and left sides. Let them tingle, and feel the sensations in your hands and body.
6. Start to bounce in one spot with your toes on the ground. Don't jump.
7. Lift your hands up high in the sky, as far as they can go.
8. Stretch to your right with your hands in the air. Then, stretch to your left with your hands in the air.
9. While both your hands are still in the air, lean back as far as you can go. Then, straighten back up.
10. Bring your hands together, and then down to your heart, and bow.

This exercise helps me when I am in long meetings or seminars and I need a break. You can do this when you are sitting on long airplane trips as well. Whenever you need a boost of energy, do this Qi Gong exercise.

To change your life, you have to change your habits. If you don't, then you will be the same as you are now in a year, ten years, or for as long as it takes for you to say enough is enough. If you want to be happier and live a fulfilling life, know that it doesn't happen overnight; you have to practice. Don't let this practice intimidate you, for it's actually fun practice that can make you feel better almost instantly. Try practicing Miracle Mornings, changing your mindset to be more positive, and doing Qi Gong to boost your energy.

PART 3 REFLECTION

- Plan out your own Miracle Morning. List what you will do and what time you will do it.
- Make a list of things you appreciate, starting with small things and working toward bigger things.
- Practice being mindful right now. Wherever you are, set a timer for one minute and close your eyes. Pay attention to everything you hear, feel, and smell around you. Concentrate on what is around you at this moment, and don't let your mind wander. Reflect on this experience.
- Do a mindset check. What mindset or attitude might be hurting you right now?
- How can you treat your current occupation like your calling? Is what you are doing really what you want to do? What do you think your calling is?
- If it was your last day on this earth, what would you be doing? What is important to you?
- Practice Qi Gong. Reflect on this experience.

PART 4

HAPPY RELATIONSHIPS

Chapter 22

OUR NEED FOR RELATIONSHIPS

I'VE BEEN DOING business for a long time. I graduated from the University of Washington with a bachelor's degree in business, concentrating on accounting and finance. I received my MBA with a concentration in finance at Keller Graduate School. From my studies and work experience, I've learned that to be successful in business, you have to have good relationships. People skills are very, very important. Having happy relationships is essential for your well-being and your mental state. Healthy relationships and advanced people skills will help you with your health, longevity, and satisfaction in life and will make your work easier and more successful. Essentially, we need happy relationships to survive and thrive.

If you have ever seen the movie *Cast Away*, you probably remember Wilson. If you haven't had the opportunity to watch it, picture this: a white volleyball with a face drawn in red paint acts as the sole friend of the protagonist, who is stuck on a desolate island.

However, Wilson is not just any volleyball. He is someone's friend. During the main character's isolation, he names the ball Wilson, talks to him, plays with him, and uses that volleyball as his companion. When he's ready to escape the island with the raft he built, he brings Wilson with him.

Unfortunately, Wilson falls into the water. The main character jumps out of the raft and tries to save Wilson. As he's trying to save him, the water pushes Wilson farther away. Unable to save Wilson, the main character shouts, "I'm sorry, Wilson!"

On the surface, most people would probably think the main character's actions were crazy. I mean, why would anyone jump into the ocean and risk their life for a volleyball? But to him, Wilson was not a volleyball. He was a friend, a loving and safe relationship in his otherwise stressful and dangerous life.

His behavior seems strange until we analyze the hierarchy of needs in our lives. Factors like water, warmth, rest, and food are the most immediate needs in our lives. Our next need is safety and security, followed by belonging and love, which is satisfied through intimate relationships and friendships. The fourth need is our esteem, prestige, and feelings of accomplishment. The fifth step, self-actualization, is achieving one's full potential, including creative activities.

So, through *Cast Away*, we see the human resilience and need to satisfy these hierarchies. When there was no one else on the island, the main character still sought out something to love and care for. This example is true of us all; we all need meaningful relationships to give us joy and purpose in life.

Hierarchy of Needs

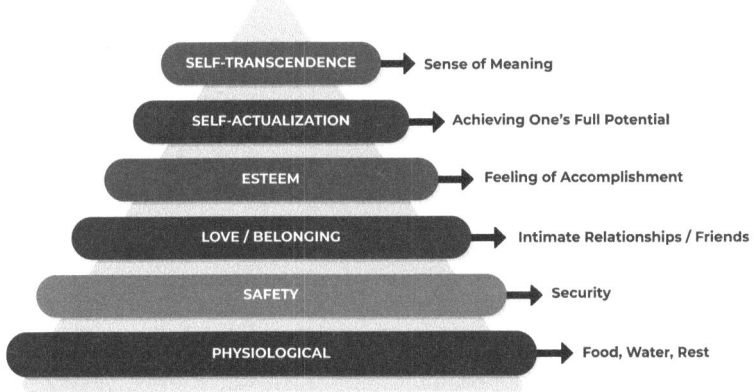

MASLOW'S HIERARCHY OF NEEDS

One of the key elements for having strong relationships is understanding that people want to be heard and validated. You have probably heard of the golden rule:

Joyful Living

"Do unto others as you want to be done to you." Well, there is a new rule called the platinum rule. The platinum rule is "treat others the way *they* want to be treated" because when you are in a relationship, you not only do what you want, but you do what other people want to do, too. How do you find out what they want and how they want to be treated? Well, you have to understand their personality type and communication style.

Chapter 23

THE FOUR PERSONALITY TYPES

AFTER ATTENDING MANY seminars and conferences, I have identified four personality types called the Four Ps: Powerful, Party, Perfectionist, and Peacemaker.

Someone with a powerful personality makes decisions quickly. They want to get to the bottom line and not beat around the bush. They are risk-takers and focus on the future. Powerful people are CEOs and leaders. They like to take charge. However, they do have some flaws. They can come off as arrogant because they have a lot of confidence. Sometimes, they seem rude or insensitive because they're not patient and they just want to get to the point. They don't want to beat around the bush and try to make everyone happy. So, they just go straight to the point.

Party people like to have fun! They live in the present moment and live life to the fullest. You can spot a party person a mile away because they like to wear colorful clothes or something different than everyone else. Party people make emotional decisions. They are risk-takers. These people are salespeople or entertainers. Their flaws often include being messy or late. They seem like they're all over the place and unorganized because they just like to party.

Peacemakers do not like conflict or change. They make slow decisions to avoid risk. They want to make sure everything is lined up before they make decisions. If you want to influence them, tell them stories about how great something is or why they should make a specific decision. For example, if I wanted to sell a peacemaker a house, I would say, "It's a great place to gather with friends and family. It will be a beautiful place to create memories." They don't like to take risks, and they don't like change. So, you have to push them to make that change. They don't want to let go of the past, so you have to sell them on the future.

Peacemakers are also givers and care about the environment and the people around them. They are like mothers of the world. They're teachers and nurses; they like to serve other people. Their flaw is that they move very slowly. They make slow decisions, and they might miss some opportunities. For example, I had a peacemaker client who wanted to buy a house. She wanted to make sure she felt comfortable buying the house, and then she wanted to ask her family for input. By the time she made the decision, the home was already gone, so she was not able to buy the house. She missed an opportunity because she makes decisions too slowly.

Perfectionists are detail-oriented. They are risk-avoidant, and they rely on data and logic. They make decisions slowly because they want all of the information beforehand. If you want to influence them, do your research and give them more data. Perfectionists are accountants, analysts, and engineers. Their flaw is that they are too detailed. They ask a lot of questions, and they might miss the big picture because they're so involved in digging into the details.

I want to give an example of a power person and a perfectionist working together. One of my friends is a power person, and she has a co-worker who is a perfectionist. The perfectionist often asks her, the power person, how to do a task. She replies, "Just do it." He asks a lot of questions, which bothers her. So, they butt heads. It's hard for them to work together because she just wants to get it done, and he wants to understand why and have all the answers before he does anything. How can they work together? If they understand each other's personality types, the power person can be more understanding of why the perfectionist is asking so many questions. The power person can answer their questions just enough to get the task done, and the perfectionist can ask just enough questions to understand the task.

Another example is a party person and a perfectionist living in the same house. A party person might be messy, and a perfectionist wants the house clean and neat. The party person might always be late, and the perfectionist will always be on time. These people need to be conscious of their different personality types in order to get along. For example, if you're a party person and your roommate is a perfectionist, be mindful of cleaning up after yourself so they can be happy. The perfectionist can be more compassionate and understand that the house will not be clean all the time.

Remember the platinum rule: Do unto others what they want, not what you want unto you. What they want is usually for people to understand them and be compassionate.

Chapter 24

FORM

IN ADDITION TO understanding someone's personality type, how can you further understand someone's uniqueness? For me, one of the best ways to deepen my understanding of someone is to FORM them. You can use this simple acronym to get to know someone on a more personal level. Remember the platinum rule: do unto others as they would want to be done to them. People usually want other people to be interested in them. So, ask about their Family, their Occupation, their Recreational activities, and their Motivation. Those four elements make up FORM and will help you make and maintain happy relationships.

Family

When you meet someone, ask them how their family is doing. Inquire about their parents and their well-being. If you don't already know, ask how big their family is, including how many siblings they have or if they have any children. Ask more about their family's background, as our families are often a core part of who we are. Getting to know this core part of a person helps foster a deeper connection.

Occupation

Once you've asked about someone's family, you can move on to their occupation. At this point, you may be able to identify the other person's personality type. If they are a CEO, they are likely a power person. Then, inquire further about how or why they followed that path. Two people with the same occupation can have different reasons, so this second question can give you some great insight into this unique person's personality.

Recreation

The third topic to address is recreation. A great, simple question to ask others is, "What do you like to do for fun?" You can tell what their personality type is by what they like to do for fun, and you can create moments for connection in which you and the other person improve your relationship with one another. If they love to travel, ask them about the trips they have gone on and why they went on those trips. If summer is coming up, ask them what their travel plans are for summer. These inquiries will show them that you care about their interests and hobbies and make them feel valued.

Motivation

Last but not least is motivation. When I do real estate, I ask my clients, "What do you like about the home?" I can often tell what type of personality they are by what they say they like about the home. If they say they love the patio where they can entertain, they're probably a party person. If they say they love all the millwork and the details in the home, then they are a perfectionist. If that's the case, I will likely give them a lot of details about what's going on in the market and more details about this house. If they just like to entertain, I would talk about how nice it would be to have their guests here, and I'd reiterate all of the great hosting space, like the patio, the great room, or the large kitchen island. Once they can see themselves living there, they might like it and want to buy the house.

Knowing someone's motivation can help foster a closer relationship and can be a gateway to their wants and needs. Understanding why someone wants, likes, or needs certain things can help you perform better in business and life as you interact with them. By understanding their motivations, you can provide better services, support, and advice in both your career relationships and personal relationships.

Chapter 25

HOLDING ON TO RELATIONSHIPS

AFTER YOU ENTER into a relationship with someone, either as a business partner or as a companion, how do you hold on to the relationship? Holding on to a relationship is like holding on to a bird; if you hold them too tightly, they might die. And if you hold them loosely, they might fly away. But if you hold them firmly yet gently and with lots of care, then they will stay with you forever. So, when you meet someone, you don't want to call them every single day and stalk them. They'll probably feel suffocated, so they'll run away from you. On the other hand, if you meet someone and you never call them, then you are out of sight, out of mind. They never see you or hear from you, so they fly away, and you don't have a relationship with them anymore.

A good relationship doesn't form in an instant. It takes time, patience, and two people who truly want to be together. I have a friend named Dan, and he told me that when he came home to his wife, he would try to hug and kiss her, but she would often say, "Oh my goodness, get off me. I have to clean the house and cook the food." Discouraged, he replied, "Okay, fine." Over time, he felt like she didn't love him. All she cared about was cooking, cleaning, and everything else she wanted to get done. But for her, she thought she was doing all that work for him and wanted him to notice and appreciate it. Over time, they started feeling resentful toward each other. They were two different personalities. He was more of a party person. When he would go to a parties, he would talk to everybody. He had so much fun. For her, she was reserved and more of a perfectionist. She would sit back in a corner or just talk to a few people. After parties, when they went home, he would often say, "Wow, that was a great party." But she would reply, "No, you took forever to get out of the party. I was ready to go home an hour ago." They had totally different personalities. One was a party person, and one was a perfectionist.

Additionally, they each had their own love language. Love languages describe how you express your feelings and how you show and receive feelings of love and appreciation. How you show your love might not be received as you intended unless you understand the other person's love language, too.

There are five different love languages:[1]

- Receiving Gifts: Buying/receiving gifts is your preferred way to show and receive love.
- Words of Affirmation: The words "I love you," "I appreciate you," "thank you," or other words of affirmation make you feel loved and help you show others you love them.

THE FIVE LOVE LANGUAGES

01	Receiving Gifts	
02	Words of Affirmation	
03	Acts of Service	
04	Quality Time	
05	Touch	

- Acts of Service: Doing things for others like cooking, cleaning the house, or any type of service is how you show love, and these acts are how you prefer to be shown you are loved by others.
- Quality Time: Spending time with your loved ones, doing things together like watching movies, going to the park or mall, or having dinner together is how you prefer to experience love.
- Touch: Hugging, holding hands, or any other physical connection makes you feel loved. You like to show others you love them by doing these things.

For example, my love language is words of affirmation. So, I say, "I love you," and "I appreciate you," a lot to my loved ones. However, if that is not their love language, they will not feel the love I am trying to communicate. In this case, I would be giving my love, but they would not be receiving it, and now, their love tank might be empty.

Do you ever hear people say, "My heart is full"? Well, that is because their love tank is full, meaning people have filled their tank by using their love language to communicate with them and let them know they are loved.

Back to my friend Dan's example—his love language was physical touch. He liked to hug and kiss his partner, but her love language was acts of service. She liked cooking and cleaning for him, and he just wanted to cuddle with her. When he was hugging and kissing her and she was cooking and cleaning for him, they both were expressing their love, but they were also becoming frustrated because neither of them felt they were receiving love in return. This is because they were essentially speaking in two different languages, and their intended messages were getting lost in translation.

Unfortunately, they got a divorce. He told me once that if he had known about love languages, they would still be married. He loved her, and she loved him. They just didn't know how to express their feelings to each other with the appropriate love language. He learned about this after the fact, but now he is remarried, and he understands love languages. He's able to shower his wife with her love language, and she is able to share his love language with him. Now, he's in a happy relationship.

Love languages are the key to holding on to relationships. You can apply this to your kids, friends, colleagues, clients/customers, and partner. When they feel like you care in their love language, they will appreciate it.

Know your loved ones' love languages so you can better express your love. If you don't, then their love tanks will be empty, and you will have a hard time maintaining a happy relationship with them. When the love tank is empty, relationship problems arise.

When your love tank is empty, the dynamics of relationships can shift dramatically, leading to misunderstandings and conflicts. Love is often likened to a reservoir; when it's full, we feel connected, valued, and secure. However, when it runs dry, feelings of neglect, resentment, and frustration can emerge. This emptiness can cloud our interactions, making it challenging to communicate effectively or empathize with our loved ones.

Understanding and acknowledging the love languages of those around us is crucial in keeping those tanks filled. Each person has a unique way of expressing and receiving love—be it through words of affirmation, acts of service, quality time, gifts, or physical touch. If we fail to recognize and engage with our loved ones' preferred love languages, we risk miscommunication. For example, a partner who values acts of service may feel unloved if we only express our affection through words, leading to feelings of disconnection and unmet needs.

When love tanks run low, relationships often suffer. Discontent can fester, leading to arguments, withdrawal, or a general sense of apathy. Conversely, by actively nurturing these connections and learning how to speak each other's love languages, we create a richer, more fulfilling relational environment. This practice fosters emotional intimacy and understanding, allowing love to flow freely and helping maintain our relationships' happiness and vitality.

But what if no one gives *you* love? Well, if you are having a hard time getting others to understand your love language, don't wait for them! You can always love yourself in the meantime! Before you can fill others' tanks, you have to fill up your own love tank. You can't serve on empty. It's not selfish to love yourself. Take care of yourself and make your happiness a priority. It's a necessity.

You are worthy. You are a creation of God, and you're perfect just the way you are. You don't need to prove to anybody who you are or what you're worth. Show yourself love by doing the things you enjoy, like going for a walk on the beach and going to the movies. Do the things that make you happy, and once you do that, your love tank will be full of self-love, and then you can fill other people's love tanks.

One of the biggest things I've learned about relationships is that you need to work on yourself first before you get into a relationship. You have to learn to love yourself before you can love another person because when your love tank is empty, issues arise, and relationships fall apart. That's why you see people act out when their love tank is not full. They take out their anger on their spouse, coworkers, friends, and themselves.

An empty love tank is what causes most relationship problems.

Consider situations like these: You are not happy with a relationship, and then you break up and go into another relationship that still has the same problems. Or, in another case, you hear a friend say, "Oh my goodness, he's such an asshole. He's so mean to me," and then she starts a new relationship and ends up with a bad guy with all the same problems. Well, this happens because you and your friend haven't fixed your own problems. You haven't filled up your own love tanks. If you don't know how to love yourself or love others, then it's very hard for you to keep a relationship.

Another way to keep a relationship is to be like a palm tree. Palm trees can withstand winds up to two hundred miles per hour winds in a storm. After a storm, many trees are usually uprooted and destroyed, but palm trees are able to withstand all the storms because they are flexible and sway side to side in the storm. They are not rigid and stiff. If they were, they would break. Being flexible means life, and stiffness means death.

Relationships are like this. If you are soft and flexible, you'll be able to prevail and keep the relationship. Are you able to listen to others? Are you able to allow your viewpoint to be challenged? Step into other people's shoes and see why they feel the way they do. You don't have to fight everything with a battle. Choose your battles wisely. If you want to influence someone, use the soft way and try being gentle first. If you use the hard way and have a big ego, it will be hard to keep the relationship or influence others.

If you have problems in your relationships, remember that they aren't perfect. Remember that your loved ones have lots of positive traits, and you should focus on those. If you focus on the positive traits, you will see more of them show up, and when you withdraw your attention from the negative traits, eventually, they will disappear.

Embracing the journey of love involves focusing on becoming the best version of ourselves in every relationship. When seeking lasting connections, it's essential to prioritize the love, joy, and connection present in the moment, allowing those feelings to flourish into new possibilities for both you and your partner. While the goal of finding enduring love is significant, fixating solely on outcomes or timelines can hinder our ability to appreciate the richness of our experiences.

If a relationship doesn't last, it's perfectly okay. What matters is that you poured your heart into it, opening yourself up to love and discovering its potential. Every relationship teaches us valuable lessons about ourselves and others, enriching our understanding and deepening our capacity for love.

So, as you navigate your relationships, focus on being the best partner you can be. And when it's time to let go, cherish the moments you shared, knowing that each experience brings you closer to new love. Embrace the journey with an open heart, and trust that each step will lead you toward the connection you seek.

Ultimately, it's essential to prioritize love in our lives, ensuring that we not only express it in ways that resonate with our loved ones but also actively seek to refill our own love tanks. By doing so, we cultivate healthier, happier relationships where everyone feels valued and connected.

Let People Go

It is important to note that, occasionally, you will not be able to solve pivotal relational problems, and you might have to let people go. The people in your life are meant to be in your journey, but not all of them are meant to stay until the end. I have had some friends who I considered my best friends, and we ended up not being friends anymore because we couldn't solve our problems, and that's okay. Some people are toxic to you, and they do not serve you in any way. So, it's better to let them go than to hold on to that particular relationship.

Instead, surround yourself with people who love you, motivate you, encourage you, and just make you feel good about being you. You have to choose to surround yourself with positive people who don't suck the energy out of you. You are who you spend time with, so choose wisely. If someone makes you feel bad about being you, then they're not a person you want to be around because they are dealing with their own battles and taking it out on you. Don't stoop down to their level, and instead, let them go peacefully. You'll have a better and happier life without them.

In summary, remember the platinum rule is to treat others the way they want to be treated. Take time to understand the four personality types—power, party, perfectionist, and peacemaker—to enhance your interactions. Strengthen your relationships by engaging in meaningful conversations about their families, occupations, recreational activities, and what motivates them (FORM). Once you've established these positive connections, nurture them by expressing love through their preferred love languages. However, just as not all seasons last forever, not all relationships are meant to endure. Like the leaves that fall from a tree, some connections serve their purpose and then naturally fade. If a relationship becomes toxic or draining, recognize that it may be time to let go and prioritize your well-being. Embrace the cycles of connection, understanding that each relationship teaches us something valuable, even if it's not meant to last.

PART 4 REFLECTION

- What is your personality type? Why do you think this?
- What is your love language?
- How are your relationships? With yourself and others?
- Which relationships in your life do you need to pay more attention to? How will you do this?
- Evaluate your relationships, which ones give you joy and which ones take more energy for you to be around. Is there anyone you need to distance yourself from? How do you feel about letting them go?

PART 5

CREATING YOUR DESTINY

Chapter 26

KARMA

IN THE INTRICATE tapestry of life, every action we take creates a ripple effect, weaving a narrative of our experiences and outcomes. This principle of cause and effect serves as the foundation for understanding how we can actively shape our destinies. Whether through the lens of the Law of Attraction, Newton's laws of motion, or the concept of karma, we see that our choices and intentions are powerful catalysts for the lives we lead.

The Law of Attraction teaches us that our thoughts and feelings attract corresponding experiences. By focusing on positive outcomes and visualizing our goals, we set in motion a chain of events that can make those desires a reality.

Isaac Newton, the renowned physicist, is well known for his laws of motion, the third of which is, "Whenever one object exerts a force on another object, the second object exerts an equal and opposite on the first."[1] When you push a pendulum, it comes back in the equal and opposite direction. What goes up, comes down. If you don't treat others with respect, they will not respect you. Newton's laws reveal that every action has an equal and opposite reaction; this highlights the importance of being mindful of our choices. The pendulum effect illustrates how our actions can swing us in one direction or another, reminding us that balance is key in navigating life's ups and downs.

Much like the Law of Attraction and Newton's third law of motion, karma encapsulates the idea that our actions—both good and bad—create consequences that shape our future. By embracing karma as a guiding principle, we can consciously choose actions that lead to positive outcomes, ultimately crafting a destiny filled with joy and fulfillment.

As Oprah Winfrey wisely said, "You want to be in the driver's seat of your own life because if you are not, life will drive you." This sentiment reflects the empowering truth that we hold the reins to our journey. By understanding the interconnectedness of cause and effect, we can harness universal laws to co-create the life we desire.

To minimize suffering and invite joy into our lives, we must first examine the root causes of our experiences.

This is where understanding karma becomes essential. Before we dive into the intricacies of karma, let's dispel some myths surrounding this powerful concept, which can serve as a valuable tool for creating the destiny you envision.

Most people think karma is a check and balance system influenced by your good and bad choices. Or people might think, "My past is equal to my future," which is not really true; that's just what fortune tellers use to tell your future because they understand your common tendencies. They use your past to predict your future, which is not a bad indicator if you keep doing exactly the same things you were doing in the past. People also think, "Oh, I can't change my destiny, so what's the point? Whatever is meant to be is meant to be, and whatever happens, happens." They have the victim mentality. They feel like life is not in their hands, and they can't control it. But that's not the case; you can control your own destiny.

People think karma is fixed and they can't do anything about it. But no, it's not fixed. You *can* change your karma. It's true that the past is already done, and you can't do anything about it. And if you keep living in the past, replaying those negative thoughts and memories, then that will be your future.

However, if you look at your past not as something that is a burden or a regret but as a stepping stone to your destination, then your future will be full of growth and good karma. The past is full of lessons. You become wiser, not wounded by failure and rejection.

And sometimes, obstacles in your past are actually gifts. Suppose someone broke up with you in the past. It was a gift because that person was not a good person for you in the future. But the next person might be the right person for you, who will respect, love, and care for you. Someone that's a better match for you. So, look at your past as a gift instead of a burden, and then you will have a brighter future. We now know that karma is not about being resigned to your past ways and looking toward the future with a heavy heart. So, what *is* karma?

Karma is about taking responsibility for oneself and the outcome of one's life without blaming parents, the economy, a boss, friends, and others for problems in life. Karma is like a boomerang, holding you accountable for everything you put out into the universe because it will come back to you. Karma is a concept that's also reflected in the Bible. Galatians 6:7 (NIV) says, "A man reaps what he sows."[2]

You reap what you sow. That's what karma is. If you have any relationship, a marriage, a boss, a friend, or whomever, and you cultivate that relationship, then you will have a long-lasting, happy relationship. But if you ignore it, you might not have a relationship anymore.

Karma is cause and effect. For example, if you have good eating habits, then you'll probably be pretty healthy. And if you eat cake once in a while, it's fine. But if you eat it too often, you might start gaining weight and developing weight-related health problems, like diabetes. The same thing happens with work. If you're lazy at work, guess what? You will not be successful. They might let you go. But if you work hard and you try to better yourself every day, then you'll be successful in your work. What you put out will come back to you.

Everything you do creates either a positive or negative consequence. You are always either creating positive karmic results or negative karmic results, depending on where you focus your thoughts, words, desires, and deeds on a daily and moment-by-moment basis. Karma cares not only about actions and consequences but also about the moral reasons or *intentions* behind actions. For example, if you donate to a charity because you want to impress others or get recognition, then you will not receive the same abundance of positive karmic results as you would if you had donated selflessly.

It is also important to note that karma accumulates not only in this lifetime but also throughout many lifetimes. I believe there's a soul within you, and after you pass, you go on to the next life. What you will get in your next life depends on how much you cultivate yourself in this life. Our karma is basically the sum of our actions, thoughts, and feelings from this life and our previous lives. Have you ever wondered why some people have very good fortune even though they are not good people?

And then some people are so nice, but luck is not on their side. Maybe this is because of their past lives.

I know some may not believe in reincarnation, so I want to share with you some information that I read that profoundly supports reincarnation. There are a lot of other resources out there on reincarnation, but this is one example.

There's a book called *Many Lives, Many Masters* by Dr. Brian Weiss. He is a Jewish Columbia University and Yale Medical School graduate and is the Chairman Emeritus of Psychiatry at the Mount Sinai Medical Center in Miami. He is a psychiatrist who helps patients with trauma through hypnotic regression. One day, he was working with a patient, and he hypnotized her to regress into her past life. She was claustrophobic and found out that she had died in a cave in one of her lives. He was shocked because he didn't believe in reincarnation. As he worked with her, he revealed many of her lifetimes and soon helped her heal all of her trauma.[3]

One day, he was taking a shower and receiving this message that he needed to write a book about this. He was apprehensive about it because he was a well-known doctor in his field and a Western doctor at that. But he knew he must write this book to tell the truth. The book ended up being a *New York Times* Best Seller.

So, what happened in your past life can spill over to your current life. Karma is an accumulation of many of our lifetimes. Our soul is permanent, and what you do during each lifetime will carry over to the next. That's why you see people gravitate to certain people or things, and some people have different skills than others. I have three kids, and they all have different personalities and interests. It's from their past lives carrying forward to this lifetime.

Furthermore, there are different kinds of karma. There's past karma, called *accumulated karma*. There's present karma, which is called *allotted karma*. And there's future karma, which is *actionable karma*.

Think of these like a retail store and its warehouse. What you produce, you put in the warehouse, and when it's ready to be sold, you put it in the retail store. So, our accumulated karma (past life) is stored in the warehouse. Our allotted karma is in the retail store, and it's affecting us right now. Whatever you do in the present, you store for the future in the warehouse, too, and when it's ready to come out, it will go into retail stores.

Remember, karma is the result of your actions, thoughts, and intentions. There are different kinds of karma spanning over multiple lifetimes. However, no matter how many mistakes you have made in the past, you can always choose to start making better choices, and this will shift your karma for the better. This means you must be intentional about everything you do, and you have to keep cultivating your karma. Much like your backyard, if you manicure it, mow it, prune it, and pull the weeds out, then it will look beautiful every month instead of looking like a forest.

Chapter 27

UNDERSTANDING KARMA

TO BETTER VISUALIZE how karma works in your life, let's analyze this graph together.

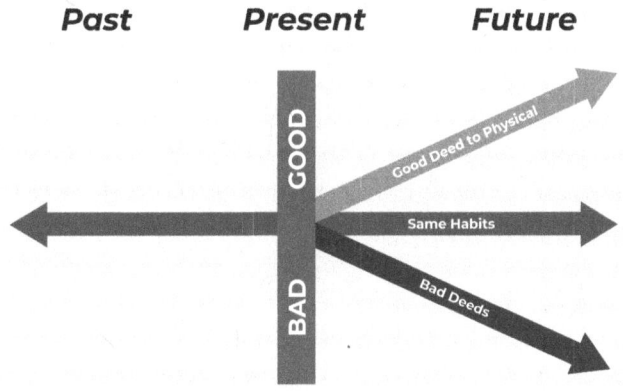

The top half of this graph represents good deeds and good life outcomes. The bottom represents bad deeds and bad life outcomes. The left of the mid-line is your past, and the right is your future. The mid-line is your present life. According to this graph—a visual representation of karma—if you do good deeds, your life will be better, but if you do bad things, your life will get worse. And if you do the exact same things today as you did yesterday and all of the days before that, then you will get the same results tomorrow. Your past will equal your future. Your life will stay the same.

People often wonder, "Why do bad things happen to me?" If something bad has happened to you, know that you're paying back bad debt, which is a good thing, and there are some lessons to be learned here. So, turn every bad thing into a positive thing, and do not dwell on your problems.

Even when you are paying back debt, you are learning lessons, and the universe is using these lessons for your benefit. When Mel Robbins is disappointed or in unfavorable situations, she follows the guidance posted on her social media accounts: "I trust life." Everything will happen in the right order for you. If one door closes, another door will open.

For example, I fractured my foot once, and I was in pain. Pain is inevitable, but suffering is my choice. I looked at it and thought, "Okay, maybe I have to pay back some bad debt because of something I did in the past and this is a lesson for me. I need to pay more attention instead of walking so fast. Maybe the universe is telling me I'm going too fast in life. I need to slow down." If I don't listen to the little whispers in life, then they're going to knock me in the head with something so I can pay attention. What happened was unfortunate, but this is my karma. I take responsibility for my actions; I don't complain, saying, "Why me?"

Sadhguru said, "Acknowledging Karma means that you see that your life is one hundred percent your doing. If you see this, you will create your life the way you want it, rather than sitting around feeling helpless, cursing your parents' genes or your current circumstances. Seeing your life as self-created rather than as an accident phenomenon—this is the basis of Karma."[1]

Like everything in life, there are events you can't control. However, you can control your response to these events. How you respond will determine the outcome of the situation.

Event + Response = Outcome

That formula was introduced to me by New York Times Best-Selling author Jack Canfield in his book *The Success Principles*. He said that you cannot change the event. However, you can change your response to the event, which then changes the outcome.[2]

For example, you could lose everything that is precious to you one day (the event). Then, you could dwell on what you lost, or you could choose to think about a

Joyful Living

new day—a clean slate (your response). Your outlook on life, your attitude, and your perspective will determine how your life unfolds (the outcome). How you see the world is what you get. When you choose to have a positive outlook and respond positively to challenging events in your life, you will have good outcomes. You have a choice every day to either suffer or be happy. Suffering is a choice made fresh every day. Your karma can't turn into suffering without your cooperation. If you're conscious, then you will probably choose happiness instead of suffering. So don't look at unfavorable events as something bad; just assume you're paying back debt or learning a lesson from whatever it is you're dealing with. You are either winning or learning in life. There's no losing in anything.

Chapter 28

HOW DO YOU CREATE GOOD KARMA?

THERE ARE MANY ways to create good karma. I will give you a few. Of course, the main one is to do good deeds. That's the easy one. Most people think good deeds are enough. They aren't. You have to have good intentions behind good actions, and you must do them joyfully. Don't do good things because you have to; do them because you want to. If you want to, then good karma will come to you, especially if you do these things consciously versus compulsively.

In *The Seven Spiritual Laws of Success*, Deepak Chopra says, "Every action generates a force of energy. When we choose actions that bring happiness and success to others, the fruit of our Karma is happiness and success."[1]

When we do good deeds for others, it brings joy not only to other people but to us, too. For example, if I buy a car, I'm excited about it for maybe two or three months or possibly as long as a year. But after that, the happiness diminishes. If you help others, you feel happy for your whole lifetime because you feel like you impacted someone's life in a significant way. These good deeds benefit others, and they can make you feel happy, too.

Another thing you have to think about when doing good deeds is the intention behind the action. Karma is not only about action; it's also about how you do it and the intention behind it. If you donate to charity for the wrong reason, then it won't bring you the same amount of good karma.

I want to share a story about three men. The three men work in real estate, and I asked them, "Why are you doing real estate?"

The first man replied, "Well, I help clients buy and sell homes, duh!"

And the second man said, "Well, I need to do it because I need to feed my family. I'm just doing this to pay the bills."

And then the third man answered, "Well, because I get to be part of their transition in life. I get to help them get their dream home or their second home or investment or whatever it is. I get to see the happiness that my clients feel because of my help."

Three different men, three different answers. It's not about what you do—it's how you do it and your intention behind it. In anything you do in life, try to do it with joy. Because if you don't enjoy it, it's not going to help you or the other person. If you feel like you're doing your job just to make ends meet, then maybe that's not the job for you. Do something that you enjoy because that will create good karma for you and your company. This way, the service you provide for others will fill them with joy.

Have you ever been to a coffee shop and the barista was very cheerful, asked how your day was, and made a good cup of coffee for you? They brightened your day, even if it was just for a moment. In the same way, when you are in a good mood, you brighten up the next person's day, and so on.

When you do things with joy, everyone benefits from them. Do what you love, and love what you do. But there's one caveat. Are you going to accept the consequences with joy? Like eating cake, for example. Yes, I love to eat it, but am I okay with accepting the consequences with joy? If I eat it too often, I can get diabetes or gain weight. If I'm not okay with these consequences, then I should be mindful about how much cake I eat. There are lots of temptations that are tough to moderate or to give up entirely. But we must be more conscious of what we do and how it affects others and ourselves.

You can create good karma by doing good deeds, with good intentions, and with joy. Be conscious and involved in everything you do in your life. When you do that, you will have ultimate freedom, and you will live a more joyful life. So, with that, I want to share a quote from Sadhguru with you. He says, "Karma means your life is your making. Karmic accumulation can either be a boost or a burden—that is your choice."[2]

In summary, karma is the cause and effect. That's all it is. If you know the results of your actions are not going to be good, then don't do it. If you are willing to joyfully accept the results of your actions, then do it.

Life is an accumulation of all the choices you have made, but you can change your future by changing the choices you make today.

Chapter 29

LIVE LIFE CONSCIOUSLY

WE HAVE TO be conscious of everything we do. In life, if we do everything consciously, it's beautiful, but if we do anything with compulsivity, it's ugly.

If you consciously cultivate relationships, then you will have good relationships. If you ignore your relationships, you might not have a relationship anymore. If you're involved with your kids' activities, then they will develop and grow and be happy. But if you're not involved with your kids, you might have depressed kids because they may disengage from activities and feel unsupported.

Furthermore, if you are conscious of what you put in your body, then you will probably have a healthy body. If you have the temptation to drink a lot of alcohol, then the next day, you will have a hangover, and that's very ugly.

This same principle is reflected by your car. If you maintain it, then you'll have a good car for a long time. But if you ignore all those warning signs to change the oil, then your car might not run anymore.

At work, if you are proactive and do your work joyfully, then your boss or clients will see that, and they will promote you or give you more business. But if you do just enough to get by, everyone will know you're just doing it for a living. They'll know they're not receiving the best service from you, and they won't reward you.

All of these examples show the importance of living life consciously. Whatever you do, do it with absolute involvement. When you are conscious about everything you're doing, then you will spread joy everywhere you go, and only then will you know the sweetness of what it means to be truly conscious in life.

This story about a fisherman perfectly describes how we should design our own destiny by living with intention. One day, a man was fishing, and it was a pretty slow day. He wasn't catching any fish, so he fell asleep. Then, a fish came. The fish yanked the fishing line, and the fisherman startled awake and grabbed the fishing rod. Since he was being careless and the fish had surprised him, he accidentally fell into the water, where he continued wrestling with the fish.

A family came by with their children, and one of the kids said to their parents, "Is that man fishing the fish, or the fish manning the man?"

Live Life Consciously

In life, we need to wake up! If we don't wake up and be more conscious, then we will continue to live on autopilot. When life gives us a fish, we'll be unprepared to catch it, and instead, it will catch us! We need to wake up and be more conscious in all that we do. When you're more conscious, you will be able to control your life and design your own destiny.

Chapter 30

WEATHERING THE STORM

THERE ARE A lot of uncertainties in the world, so how can we get through adversity? Well, I want to start off by telling you a little story.

There was a girl who was struggling with life. She had relationship problems, she was not doing well in school, and she was gaining weight with all the stress life had put on her. One day, she went to her mom and asked, "Why is life so tough?" Her mom took her into the kitchen and brought out three pots. She put an egg in the first pot, coffee beans in the second, and a carrot in the third, each with some water, and placed the pots on the stovetop, then turned on the stove to let the water boil. After twenty minutes, she put the three items into their own bowls.

She asked her daughter to take a look at each one of them and tell her what she observed.

First, she instructed her daughter, "Feel the carrot."

"It's soft and mushy," her daughter replied.

"Try to break the egg," the mom said, and the daughter observed that the egg was now hard.

Finally, she asked the daughter to sip the coffee. The daughter smiled as she inhaled the aroma of the coffee and took a sip. "So, what's the point?"

The mother said, "Each of the objects faced adversity, but each one reacted differently. The carrot went in strong and hard but softened in the boiling water. This represents those who want to conquer the world—they go in strong and excited, but when they experience their first rejection or failure, they often wither like a flower in the hot sun.

"The egg's outer layer was thin and fragile, but after sitting in the boiling water, the inside became hardened. This represents people who are outwardly sensitive and fragile. However, when they face hardship, they become bitter, hard, and have lots of hatred inside.

"The coffee bean, however, is unique. It came in hard and ended hard, but after being immersed in the boiling water, the bean changed the water instead of the water changing it! This represents the type of people who, no matter what gets thrown at them, are able to adapt to or change the environment for the better. They look for the positive sides of things. When life throws them a lemon, they make lemonade!"

The mother then asked, "Which one are you? When adversity knocks on your door, how do you respond? Are you a carrot, an egg, or a coffee bean?"[1]

You see, life is going to come at us no matter what. There are things that come into our lives that we can't control, like changes in the economy. What are you going to do when the storm hits? Are you going to cry about it, get mad at it, or learn how to dance in the rain?

I am going to share with you not only how to survive but also how to thrive in the midst of a storm.

MAP Your Way Out of the Storm

While reflecting on all that I had learned in order to write this book, I came up with an idea I call MAP: Meditate, Adapt, and be Positive.

First, let's talk about *meditation*. I like to think of meditation like a snow globe. When you shake it, there's a flurry of snow inside the globe that covers the scenery. However, when you put it down, everything settles, and you can see what's in the snow globe. So, if we keep overanalyzing and overthinking, wondering what's going to happen to the economy, our family, and our career, then our vision is clouded—the "snow" covers the scenery. But if we sit still, our minds settle, and we can more easily see the answers to our questions or problems. We might even find some creativity and brainstorm ideas on how to do things better. In this way, meditation helps you become better.

The next step in MAP is to **adapt** to the situation. It is debated whether or not Charles Darwin once said, "It's not the strongest of the species that survives, nor the most intelligent that survives; it's the one that is the most adaptable to the change." Regardless of the quote's true origin, the wisdom of these words still stands.

During the COVID-19 pandemic, KIRO News showed how one business owner adapted to the pandemic restrictions. This man was suffering because his coffee shop was in downtown Bellevue, Washington. There are lots of businesses around there, but during the pandemic, there was less foot traffic because a lot of people were working from home. So, the business owner began brainstorming about how he could attract more foot traffic.

He noticed there were lots of farmers' markets nearby, and he asked himself, "Why aren't we using them? I mean, there are farmers who want to sell to consumers, but the farmers' markets are not open right now, and they need a storefront to sell their produce." He realized that those farmers could sell their produce and products in his coffee shop, and the consumers who wanted local produce could go to the coffee shop, thus increasing his foot traffic! Talk about being a coffee bean in the face of adversity! This guy thought outside the box. Instead of closing his shop, he increased his sales and helped his community. Because of his adaptability, he was able to weather the storm with his business.

Last but not least, be ***positive***. I know some people say that staying positive is easier said than done. These people are often full of fear and doubt. Fear can hold us back, especially in uncertain times. People who have been wounded by their careers, finances, or personal relationships are afraid of being let down again, so they say life is unfair, and they doubt that things will change for the better. With that mindset, they surrender hope and positive optimism. Hope and optimism allow you to embrace uncertainty. Optimism is not naive. It is the belief that the future is bright. It's not the denial of reality. So, we have to believe and have hope that things will be better because if we don't, we will suffer through the storm.

Dictate your Destiny

Your beliefs shape your thoughts, which in turn create your emotions. These emotions drive the inspired actions you take, ultimately producing results that reinforce your beliefs. So, how can you shift your beliefs to cultivate more positive outcomes?

The first step is to rewire your belief system.

Consider the Pixar movie *Inside Out 2*. In the film, Riley's belief system forms the core of her identity. She grapples with thoughts like "I am a good person" or "I am not good enough." When she doubts her abilities, such as during her hockey game, it affects her performance. This illustrates the adage: "If you think you can or you think you can't, you're probably right." Her emotions guide her actions—when Joy leads, she thrives; when Anxiety takes over, she falters.

This principle extends to everyday choices, such as why people buy expensive cars like Ferraris. The decision often stems from how these cars make them feel despite the logical drawbacks, such as higher costs and fuel consumption. Similarly, we indulge in chocolates and sweets, fully aware of their health risks, simply because they bring us joy.

So, how can we gain control over our emotions? It begins with our beliefs. By consciously shaping these beliefs, we can alter our thoughts, which then influence our emotions, actions, and results, thereby reinforcing our new, positive beliefs.

You might wonder, "How can I believe in something when I haven't achieved it yet?" The notion that "seeing is believing" holds some truth, but it's essential to recognize that our minds often cannot distinguish between reality and imagination.

If you feel overwhelmed by the effort to change, try the Power of 2% method. For instance, if your goal is to run a marathon, starting with two hours of running each day might lead to soreness and discouragement. Instead, begin with just five minutes, then gradually increase your time by two percent, then two percent more. This incremental approach builds confidence, making it easier to believe in your ability to achieve greater goals.

Just like teaching a child to read, where you wouldn't start at a level far beyond their ability, focus on manageable challenges. Start where you are, and then gradually push your limits. This fosters confidence, propelling you toward your aspirations. With each small success, your belief in your potential grows, paving the way for greater achievements.

At any given moment, you're in one of two states. One is your positive state, and the other is your negative state. The positive state is when you are hopeful, loving, joyful, excited, curious, and peaceful. In the negative state, you're bored, angry, frustrated, sad, or fearful.

One of my friends said she is always in a negative state. She can't get it out of her head, and she doesn't believe that she belongs in our group of friends. I asked her, "Are you a spiritual person?"

She said yes, so I replied, "Then how did God put you in a place where you don't belong?"

She paused and had an aha moment. "I belong everywhere I am."

Nothing changed except for her belief about herself and where she belonged, but this change made a huge difference in her perception of reality and her inspired actions going forward. She reconnected with her positive state. So, next time you face adversity, assess if your thoughts are negative or positive. If they are negative, know that you can change your mindset and your perception of reality. Believe that things will get better in the long run. You are smart, worthy, and belong wherever you are.

Don't think, "Why me?" and play the victim. Instead, adopt a positive, curious mindset and wonder, "What can I learn from this?" If you look from that perspective instead of being mad, you will be able to move on and be at peace. Without a positive mindset that allows you to move on, you will never truly get through the storms in life. Look for the positive in every situation, and practice developing beliefs that set you up for success.

Chapter 31

IT'S OKAY TO BE ANGRY

AS A CHILD, my son was aggressive sometimes. If he wanted something, he would bite or pinch his twin sister. I tried to talk to him, but nothing worked. I talked to a mental health professional, and she said that it's okay to be angry, but she advised me to find a space for him where he could let out his anger, such as a corner, so he could hit, pout, or shout. Then, after he calmed down, I could talk to him, and maybe he would feel better because he needed that time and space to breathe.

It's okay for you to be angry at your situation—positivity is not possible all the time. Sometimes, we need to feel our anger and let it out. Try to be conscious of that feeling, take a step back, and breathe before you take your next action. We're all human. People say or do things that will piss us off. We have to acknowledge that, breathe, take a moment, and then act. When we react compulsively, that's when problems arise.

I went to a birthday party for one of my friends, and there was a lady there who said she did something that she was not proud of. I want to share that example, and as you read, keep this question in mind: If it happened to you, what would you do?

She was in line at a grocery store, and two men were in front of her. They were together, and they were just talking. Martin Luther King Day was coming up, and one of the guys said, "Hey, do you have Martin Luther King Day off?"

The other replied, "Yeah, but that's a stupid holiday."

From behind them, she exclaimed, "What?"

The man turned around, looked at her, and said, "If six more people get assassinated, I'll have a week off."

She's a black female, and she was so pissed. I mean, she didn't even think. She just slapped the hell out of that guy until he was on the floor. She was so mad, thinking, "How could you say that?"

So, of course, the police came. We are all human, so we will all experience anger. But when people do things to make you pissed off, take a breath and step back before you take the next action. Otherwise, you could let your anger rule your actions, and you could end up in a similar situation as the woman in the story. She had to deal with the police and other angry people.

So, ask yourself if you have ever been in a situation where you let your anger get the best of you, and using your knowledge from this book, brainstorm how you could have handled the situation better.

Remember, always learn the lessons. Do not dwell on the guilt and shame of what you did. Don't participate in cancel culture. Do not cancel someone because they did something wrong or because they're human and they reacted. In the Church, they always have space for you to repent. If people repent, then they acknowledge what they did wrong, and they apologize. So, as long as they know they did wrong, and they apologize and are remorseful, I will have grace. I encourage you, too, to have grace for yourself and others and acknowledge that anger is a part of being human, and we all must work hard to express that anger appropriately.

Chapter 32

THE BUTTERFLY EFFECT

THE BUTTERFLY EFFECT is the idea that small things can have non-linear impacts on complex systems, meaning an event can take place that causes another seemingly unrelated event in a different time or place. The concept is imagined with a butterfly flapping its wings and causing a typhoon. Of course, a single act, like the butterfly flapping its wings, is highly unlikely to cause a typhoon. However, the point still remains that your actions have both intended and unintended consequences that can compound and ripple out to affect the world.

The butterfly effect illustrates that if you do small, good habits over time, you can have a huge positive impact on your life and others' lives. For example, if I were to give you the choice of three million dollars today or one penny that doubles every day for thirty-one days, which would you rather have? Most people would pick the three million dollars. But due to the power of compound interest, you would actually have more money at the end of the month if you chose the penny! Much like the penny, your happiness will compound, and as you accumulate happiness habits, your life will get better.

Likewise, doing small, good deeds daily for others can have compounding effects on their lives that may brighten their days and uplift their spirits, affecting their inspired actions. These actions will have consequences you could never have predicted and could continuously spread joy in a large ripple, all from your small acts and your joyful, positive mindset.

People always say to think big, but you don't need to. Start small because every building you've seen started with one brick; every marathon runner thinks about the next step, not the next twenty-six miles; and tennis players think about one point at a time, not all three matches. The power of small steps is that over time, consistent, persistent small steps make overwhelming differences in life.

Chapter 33

FULFILLMENT

HAVE YOU EVER met someone who was very successful and had everything they ever wanted, but they were not happy? It was because they hadn't reached the highest level of the hierarchy of needs. They reached their full potential, but there's one more level in the hierarchy to true fulfillment. Fulfillment has many levels, which can be explained through Maslow's Hierarchy of Needs.[1] As you can see in the image, the lowest levels of fulfillment are physiological and safety, which revolve around food, water, rest, and security. Once you have acquired these basic needs, making intimate relationships will help you achieve the next level, called love/belonging. But don't stop there. To continue to be fulfilled, you must reach the esteem level by doing things that make you feel accomplished. From there, people strive to reach their full potential in the self-actualization stage. But true fulfillment comes once you establish a sense of meaning in the self-transcendence stage. This is not easily attainable, but the effort is worth it. This level is when you want to selflessly contribute to the world. Self-transcendence is finding your why and knowing that life is not about you. We are all connected; we are all one entity. When you believe we are all one consciousness and help others in the same manner that you help yourself, you leave the planet better than you came. That's my purpose—to try to leave the planet better than I came.

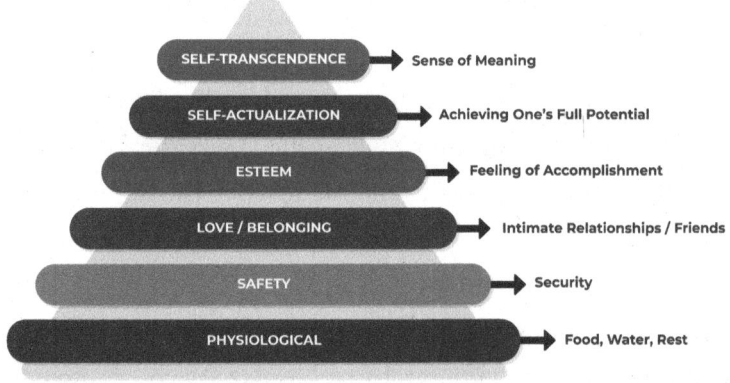

MASLOW'S HIERARCHY OF NEEDS

Everything we do, even the smallest action, has a ripple effect. So, before you take on any role or pursue your dreams, remember that whatever you do is either pushing humanity forward or moving us back.

For example, researcher Tom Chi was asked by a beverage company to market their new flavor to teens. He told them that soda contributes to obesity and diabetes. They knew that, but they dodged his concern. He knew that he didn't want to contribute to this project and its effects on the world. So, he turned down a $250,000 project because it conflicted with his values.[2] He cared about the human race. He wanted his work to bring positive change. If he believes a project won't bring positive change, he won't work on it. That's how much he cares about what he does for a living. True success and joy do not depend on how much money you make but on what you give and how you selflessly impact the lives you touch.

We are all connected one way or another and depend on each other more than we know. We are like cells in the human body. Everything you create and every action you take impacts others. So, are you a cancer cell or a healthy cell? Does your work positively impact humanity, or is it like a disease? Are you making the world sicker or better?

As you strive to be fulfilled, consider those around you, but also enjoy the journey. Even though it might take a while to reach the self-transcendence level, don't forget to enjoy each level because we only have so much time in this life. There is still joy to be found in each level if you have the right mindset. If you are at the love/belonging level, enjoy creating new relationships. Appreciate what you do have and how far you have come,

Joyful Living

and most importantly, always give what you can. Keep this mindset as you strive to reach each new level, and you will achieve self-transcendence.

Chapter 34

REAL HAPPINESS

LIVE YOUR JOYFUL life now. Don't wait until you get the house, that car, the kids you wanted, or that career, and then try to be happy. I want you to be happy now and be present in the moment because right now is all there is. The past is already over, the future is not here yet, and you can only control what is happening here and now.

    You do not live forever. So, enjoy the moment you have right now and appreciate all the things you have. Some people take what they have for granted, and then once it's gone, they start appreciating what they had or regretting that they didn't cultivate that relationship or part of the life they once had. But why not appreciate what you have right now? When you appreciate what

Joyful Living

you have and feel totally blessed, you will get more blessings.

Then, everything in your life will fall into place. You will be more productive and creative, your relationships will improve, your health will get better, and you will have more energy. Essentially, you will reach your full potential.

The practices in this book can act like shock absorbers in a car, assisting you on your journey to happiness. Practices such as meditation and practicing appreciation can help absorb the shock of adversity, disappointment, or setbacks. With these practices, you can get back on track faster and get to where you want to go. In life, things are going to happen. Someone is going to upset you, or things aren't going to go your way. However, by using these practices to absorb the shock, you can continue to grow and move on.

Going forward, be conscious and awake, and don't settle with the status quo of life. If you don't intentionally plan your life, then other people will plan your life. You have this one life; why not live it to the fullest of what you want instead of what other people want?

Lastly, lead by example. Be an example of joy, love, and positive energy. Love yourself, work on yourself, and practice all these things I shared with you, and then you can spread joy.

That is what I hope for you: to be happy, live out your dreams, and spread joy!

Chapter 35

CONCLUSION

IN CLOSING, REMEMBER that joy is not just a fleeting feeling; it is a powerful foundation for a fulfilling life. By cultivating happiness within yourself, you unlock the potential for abundance in every area of your life—relationships, well-being, spirituality, and your unique journey. Embrace the idea that joy fuels kindness, creativity, productivity, and vitality.

Life is not merely about following the expected path; it's about exploring the unknown and crafting a story that resonates with your true self. Let each day be an opportunity to seek out positivity and be the beacon of light you wish to see in the world. As you nurture your happiness, you'll inspire those around you, creating ripples of joy in your community and beyond.

Joyful Living

Do what you love, and let passion guide your actions. When your pursuits are rooted in love, life transforms into a fulfilling adventure rather than mere labor. Just like a seed needs care to grow, so too does your joy require nurturing. With love, everything flourishes.

Always remember: life is a journey, not a destination. Relish every moment, for the present is the only time that truly exists. Don't wait for happiness to arrive; cultivate it now. Live the life you love, and watch as everything unfolds beautifully around you. Embrace the adventure, savor the joy, and create a legacy of love and happiness for generations to come.

PART 5 REFLECTION

- Reflect on your understanding of karma.
- Have you ever had something happen, either good or bad, that seemed to have no explanation? Explain. Do you think this could have been based on your karma?
- What small changes can you make as you go about your day to improve your destiny?
- In what aspects of your life are you living on autopilot?
- Think of a problem you are facing. Journal or meditate on this problem. Consider if there are any positive aspects in this situation, and then write out a plan to adapt to the situation or find a solution. Try to have a more positive mindset about it.
- Brainstorm how to safely and responsibly deal with your anger. Where could you go to de-escalate? Who could you talk to? What could you do to bring yourself comfort without harming others?
- What practices can you apply daily to be happier and at peace? Try them out for a week and see how they make you feel.

Find joy in the journey.

Additional Reading and Happiness Resources

Ask and It Is Given: Learning to Manifest Your Desires by Esther and Jerry Hicks
Miracle Morning by Hal Elrod
The Happiness Advantage by Shawn Achor
The Power of Now by Eckhart Tolle
The Success Principles by Jack Canfield
The Seven Spiritual Laws of Success by Deepak Chopra
Sattva, Calm, and Abraham Hick's fifteen-minute meditations

Notes

Introduction
1. Eckhart Tolle, *The Power of Now* (New World Library, 2000), 11.

Chapter 1
1. Shawn Achor, *The Happiness Advantage* (Crown Currency, 2010).
2. Ibid.

Chapter 4
1. "Where Focus Goes, Energy Flows," 2024, Tonyrobbins.com.

Chapter 6
1. "Trading Expectations for Appreciation," 2021, https://www.tonyrobbins.com/podcast/trade-expectations-appreciation/.

Chapter 8
1. Achor, *The Happiness Advantage,* n.p.
2. Ibid.
3. Ibid.
4. Ibid.

Chapter 9
1. Sadhguru, *Karma* (Penguin Random House Australia, 2021).
2. Prince Ea, "Everybody Dies, But Not Everybody Lives" (Facebook, 2016).

Chapter 13
1. "Whatever the Mind Can Conceive and Believe, It Can Achieve," wanderlustworker.com.

Chapter 14
1. "Destiny By Design Free Webinar: Get Unstuck & Dream Big Again!" DreamBigWithThach.com/dbd.

Chapter 16
1. Hal Elrod, *Miracle Morning* (BenBella Books, 2023)"
2. Ibid.
3. Ibid.
4. Ibid.

Chapter 18
1. "14 Amazing Benefits of Meditation That Can Actually Rewire Your Brain," Science of People, 2024, https:/www.scienceofpeople.com/meditation-benefits/.
2. Ellen Langer, *Counterclockwise: Mindful Health and the Power of Possibility* (Hodder Paperback, 2010).
3. Ibid.
4. Deepak Chopra, *The Healing Self* (Harmony, 2020).

Chapter 19
1. Achor, *The Happiness Advantage*, 64.

Chapter 20
1. Peter Salovey and Amy Wrzesniewski. "Yale Talk: Conversations with Peter Salovey." Yale Talk, Episode 25, 28 Feb. 2022.
2. Achor, *The Happiness Advantage,* n.p.

Chapter 25
1. Gary Chapman, *The 5 Love Languages* (Northfield Publishing, 2015).

Chapter 26
1. "Newton's Laws of Motion," NASA, 2023, https://www1.grc.nasa.gov/beginners-guide-to-aeronautics/newtons-laws-of-motion/#.
2. Galatians 6:7 (NIV).

3. Brian Weiss, *Many Lives, Many Masters* (Fireside, 1988).

Chapter 27
1. Sadhguru, *Karma*, n.p.
2. Jack Canfield, *The Success Principles: How to Get from Where You Are to Where You Want to Be* (William Morrow Paperbacks, 2006).

Chapter 28
1. Deepak Chopra, *The Seven Spiritual Law of Success* (Amber-Allen Publishing, 2015).
2. Sadhguru, *Karma*, n.p.

Chapter 30
1. "Are You a Carrot, Egg, or Coffee Bean?" Weekly Wisdom Blog, 2022, https://www.weeklywisdomblog.com/post/are-you-a-carrot-egg-or-coffee-bean.

Chapter 33
1. "The New Hierarchy of Needs – Maslow's Lost Apex," 2018, https://jessiechristian.medium.com/the-new-hierarchy-of-needs-maslows-lost-apex-5e51031ce3fb.
2. Vishen Lakhiani, *The Buddha and the Badass: The Secret Spiritual Art of Succeeding at Work* (Rodale Books, 2020).

About the Author

Liên Ngoc Ngū has been an energetic spiritual teacher for many years. Her former occupation was as a Sr. Financial and Business Analyst. She received her bachelor's degree from the University of Washington and Master of Business Administration from Keller Graduates of Devry University.

Liên has presented at temples, communities, and businesses. One of her biggest speaking engagements was at the Taiwanese American Professional National Conference in Seattle. As a result of her passion for learning, growing, and sharing with others, she has been able to help many people find peace within themselves and reach their goals. Through her principles and strategies,

Joyful Living

people are able to apply what they learn, create the life they want, and live a joyful life!

Liên enjoys reading, meditating, doing yoga, traveling, spending time with her family and friends, and helping the community. She lives happily in Bellevue, WA, with her husband and three kids.